Taking It to the Streets

TAKING IT TO THE STREETS

The Role of Scholarship in Advocacy
and Advocacy in Scholarship

EDITED BY LAURA W. PERNA

Johns Hopkins University Press
Baltimore

© 2018 Johns Hopkins University Press
All rights reserved. Published 2018
Printed in the United States of America on acid-free paper

2 4 6 8 9 7 5 3 1

Johns Hopkins University Press
2715 North Charles Street
Baltimore, Maryland 21218-4363
www.press.jhu.edu

Library of Congress Cataloging-in-Publication Data
Names: Perna, Laura W., editor.
Title: Taking it to the streets : the role of scholarship in advocacy and advocacy in
scholarship / edited by Laura W. Perna.
Description: Baltimore : Johns Hopkins University Press, 2018. | Includes
bibliographical references and index.
Identifiers: LCCN 2017038116| ISBN 9781421425467 (paperback : alk. paper) |
ISBN 9781421425474 (electronic) | ISBN 1421425467 (paperback : alk. paper) |
ISBN 1421425475 (electronic)
Subjects: LCSH: Education, Higher—Research. | Education, Higher—Social aspects.
| Learning and scholarship—Social aspects. | Social advocacy. | Social change.
Classification: LCC LB2326.3 .T27 2018 | DDC 378.007—dc23
LC record available at https://lccn.loc.gov/2017038116

A catalog record for this book is available from the British Library.

Special discounts are available for bulk purchases of this book. For more information,
please contact Special Sales at 410-516-6936 or specialsales@press.jhu.edu.

Johns Hopkins University Press uses environmentally friendly book materials,
including recycled text paper that is composed of at least 30 percent
post-consumer waste, whenever possible.

To all those whom academic researchers try to serve through their work, and to all those who provide the love, guidance, and other support that academic researchers need to engage in and sustain their efforts

contents

Taking It to the Streets

chapter 1

Introduction

Taking It to the Streets

LAURA W. PERNA

Higher education is critical to the economic and social well-being of individuals and our society (Baum, Ma, and Payea 2013). Moreover, the importance of higher education is growing, as available jobs increasingly require some level of postsecondary education (Carnevale and Rose 2015; Carnevale, Smith, and Strohl 2010). But the opportunity to realize the benefits of higher education varies, as college-related outcomes differ based on demographic characteristics, place of residence, and K–12 and higher education institutions attended (Baum et al. 2013; Cahalan et al. 2016; Perna and Finney 2014).

The paragraph you just read cites various sources to support a particular argument: there are deep and persisting inequities within our nation's educational systems and structures (e.g., Perna 2006). But not all observers make the same argument or draw the same conclusions. The depth of differences in perspectives about equity, inclusiveness, and social change in US higher education is suggested by responses to actions taken by the Trump administration. While some support the selection of Betsy DeVos as secretary of the Department of Education and the issuance of executive orders banning travel to the United States from predominantly Muslim nations—as well as restrictions on free speech on campus, elimination of protections for transgender students, and reductions in federal support for student financial aid, research, and other federally supported programs—others have voiced strong opposition (Stripling 2017).

Many faculty, researchers, and graduate students conduct research with the goal of advancing equity, inclusiveness, and social change in higher education (Perna 2016). Although this research is necessary, merely conducting it is not sufficient to create policy change. Advancing these goals also requires academic researchers to connect research and policy.

Most would agree about the utility of disseminating research results to audiences beyond the traditional scholarly community in order to influence policy. There is less agreement about whether and how academic researchers should be advocates for equity, inclusiveness, and social change. As faculty, scholars, and graduate students, we have the academic freedom to study topics and problems about which we care deeply. And we may choose when and how we engage in efforts to advance equity, inclusiveness, and social change. But is there a difference between being a researcher and being an advocate? When social media provides a platform for anyone to express an opinion about equity, inclusiveness, and social change, what differentiates academic researchers from other individuals who have opinions about these issues? Is it too naïve to believe that "when we are armed with research, we [academic researchers] should be a much more powerful force for change" (Perna 2016, 332)?

Purpose of This Volume

This volume is intended to advance dialogue about the connections among research, advocacy, and policy from the perspective of academic researchers. In addition to this introduction, the volume includes sixteen essays in which nationally and internationally recognized higher education scholars offer their views. The invited authors have pursued different professional pathways and employed different methodological approaches. But each brings great passion and deep commitment to advancing equity, inclusiveness, and social change in higher education—and each has made noteworthy contributions to these issues over the course of their careers.

Essays in this volume reflect on the contributions that academic researchers have—and have not—made to advancing equity, inclusiveness, and social change in higher education (e.g., Minor, Chang) and offer examples of the use of research in policymaking processes (e.g., Heller, Marginson, Solorzano). The authors describe how they have understood connections among research, advocacy, and policy in different roles (e.g., Marginson, Stanley, Austin, Rhoades), as well as their personal motivations for doing their work (e.g., Bensimon, Crazy Bull, Harper, Goldrick-Rab, Solorzano). The essays offer frameworks for making decisions about our work (e.g., Rhoades, Tierney, Kezar) and suggestions for how to improve connections among research, advocacy, and policy (e.g., Gamoran, Oakes and Berryman).

As several authors stress (e.g., Kezar, Oakes and Berryman, Rhoades, Tierney), individual scholars decide whether, when, and how to engage in public scholarship. All of the authors in this volume have made the "professional, ethical, and political choices," as Gary Rhoades discusses, to do so. While all acknowledge their commitment to high-quality research, only some of the authors articulate a distinction between research and advocacy. By including individuals with diverse backgrounds and viewpoints, the volume is intended to provide a thought-provoking portrayal of the many ways scholars at various career stages distinguish between research and advocacy in their efforts to advance equity, inclusiveness, and social change in higher education.

Although this introduction begins with a brief argument for advancing equity, inclusiveness, and social change, justifying these goals is not the purpose of this volume. Rather, the volume is intended to collect insights from scholars who are committed to these goals and encourage reflection about such questions as, What is the role of higher education research in informing higher education policymakers and practitioners about the need for policies that address these issues? Do higher education researchers differentiate themselves from advocates? How, why, and when should higher education researchers be public intellectuals?

Guiding Orientations

The essays in this volume illustrate differences among academic researchers in the answers to these questions. As academic researchers, our answers to these questions depend, at least in part, on how we conceptualize our work and define our priorities. Three underlying orientations inform how I try to advance equity, inclusiveness, and social change in higher education.

Orientation #1: Focus on Policy Analysis Rather than Politics

One guiding orientation is an interest in advancing equity, inclusiveness, and social change as a policy analyst rather than as a politician. With the aspiration of improving equity in opportunity at the local level, I took my bachelor's degrees in economics and psychology and accepted my first professional job working for a local elected official in Hudson County, New Jersey. At the time, the economy of this densely populated metropolitan area (which is home to Jersey City and other small cities, and located across the Hudson River from Manhattan) was transitioning from manufacturing to financial services. My charge was to consider what local government might do to ensure that the county's higher education providers equipped long-time residents with the education and training required for the jobs that were being created.

This responsibility increased my interest in—and understanding of—the role of public policy in creating higher education opportunities and outcomes. It also provided useful insights into the dependence of policy reform on different players, roles, and expertise, or what Simon Marginson (this volume) calls "a division of labor" between politician and researcher. Politicians are motivated to take actions that will help them get elected and re-elected, whereas researchers are trained to produce analyses that inform understanding of the problems as well as the effects and implications of potential policy solutions. With the goal of producing the types of analysis that would help policymakers advance the "right" policies, I enrolled in the master's degree program in public policy at the University of Michigan and stayed on to earn my doctorate in education.

Orientation #2: Identify the Best Solution from Data and Research

A second orientation that guides my work came through my employment with the Frederick D. Patterson Research Institute of the United Negro College Fund (UNCF). With my dissertation advisor and supervisor Michael Nettles, our primary charge was to produce three comprehensive data books that documented trends in the status and experiences of African Americans relative to other racial/ethnic groups at all levels of education, from pre-kindergarten through adult. These descriptive analyses generated an endless list of researchable questions and improved my knowledge of the ways that existing datasets may be used, at least as a starting point, for addressing important questions and identifying potential solutions.

Through interactions with the staff at UNCF and other Washington, DC-based associations, I also learned the questions that policymakers are asking and want answered. But, like Marginson, over time I became uncomfortable advancing potential policy changes from within an organization with a defined agenda. I too came to believe that "we did not have all the answers." I learned that I wanted to identify preferred policy solutions based on an understanding of the underlying contextual issues and a thorough review of prior research, and by conducting independent research and analysis on the questions I believed were most important.

Orientation #3: Recognize the Roles and Responsibilities of Our Positions

A third orientation pertains to the multiple roles that faculty and academic researchers hold. Different roles allow us to connect research and advocacy to advance policy in different ways. As a faculty member at the University of

Maryland, College Park, and now at the University of Pennsylvania, I have focused my scholarly agenda on understanding how to ensure that all students—regardless of demographic background or place of residence—have the opportunity to enroll in and benefit from high-quality higher education. My research agenda has developed over time to consider multiple dimensions of this broad topic, using both quantitative and qualitative methodologies and different theoretical lenses and conceptual models.

Decisions about how to disseminate my work reflect my understanding of the requirements to achieve tenure and promotion within the academy. Especially as a graduate student and assistant professor, I prioritized activities that would secure my longer-term future and status as an academic. Not only did I want to achieve tenure and the ranks of associate and full professor, but I also needed time to learn the norms of academic publishing.

As I have progressed in my career (and especially now as a full professor), I have become more proactive in disseminating findings in outlets beyond those that reach only other academics and are most valued in the tenure and promotion processes. Like other authors in this volume, I have offered testimony to committees in the US Senate and House of Representatives about the changes in policy and practice that are needed to eliminate persistent barriers to higher education opportunities and outcomes for underrepresented and underserved students. I deliver addresses to meetings of academic researchers as well as higher education leaders, administrators, and policymakers, and I write policy briefs, blogs, and op-eds. I also make myself available to journalists operating on tight deadlines to offer background information and on-the-record commentary on issues that fall within my expertise.

I believe these opportunities have happened—especially as my career has advanced—at least in part because of relationships and networks. While at UNCF and the University of Maryland, I made efforts to meet, talk with, and learn from colleagues working at policy associations in Washington, DC. These interactions led to collaborations on policy briefs and invitations to serve on various advisory groups. At Penn, I have made local connections, especially with colleagues in other parts of the university (including the Netter Center for Community Partnerships and the Institute for Urban Research) and at Philadelphia-based college access organizations. These relationships have provided opportunities to not only share research results but also better understand how college opportunities and outcomes play out in local communities.

As faculty, we also advance connections between research, advocacy, and policy through teaching and advising graduate students and junior colleagues. Like Donald E. Heller (this volume), I too was fortunate as a graduate student and junior scholar to have mentors who modeled efforts to connect research, advocacy, and policy, and broadened my networks to include non-academic users of research. If we value connections among research, advocacy, and policy, then, as faculty members, we are responsible for ensuring that graduate students and junior colleagues have the skills, understandings, and relationships required to make these connections.

We also have opportunities to connect research, advocacy, and policy through the roles we assume over the course of our careers. In their essays, Gary Rhoades and Ann E. Austin describe how they have connected research, advocacy, and policy in their positions with the American Association of University Professors and the National Science Foundation, respectively. Christine A. Stanley reflects on how she applies research findings to call attention to bias in promotion and tenure discussions.

As 2015 president of the Association for the Study of Higher Education (ASHE), my choice of conference theme, Inequality and Higher Education, reflected my beliefs about the policy issues that are important for a community of scholars to address (Rhoades 2006). My program chair, Matthew Mayhew, and I also chose to highlight issues pertaining to indigenous peoples through our selection of Cheryl Crazy Bull, president of the American Indian College Fund, as a keynote speaker, and the inclusion of indigenous ceremonies to open and close the conference. These choices may be characterized as political, or politicized, as they reflect our preferencing of particular issues over the many other potential topics that could have been featured.

We also have opportunities to connect research, advocacy, and policy in our on-campus roles. As chair of the faculty senate at Penn, I have had the opportunity to provide input to Penn's administration on issues of importance to, and from the perspective of, the faculty, including Title IX and sexual assault, student mental health and wellness, and student and faculty diversity. While these efforts have largely involved behind-the-scenes discussions, a few actions have been more public. In November 2016, in the days following the presidential election, Black freshmen on Penn's campus were targeted via social media with horrific, racist messages. In response, the faculty senate issued a statement condemning "racism and bigotry on and off our campus" and committing "to the advancement of equity, inclusiveness, and constructive dialogue on our campus" ("Statement" 2016) and led a march of solidarity for Black Penn students, faculty, and staff. In February 2017, we issued a statement opposing President Donald J. Trump's executive order on immigration and organized a gathering of solidarity for affected members of our community. The faculty senate leadership deemed these and other actions as necessary responses to violations of higher education's core principles and values, including equity and inclusiveness.

As faculty, we enact and make policy through our institutional service and when we make decisions about admissions to graduate programs, faculty hiring and promotion, and other matters (Perna 2016). While some decisions may reflect insights we have gleaned from research, others reflect our personal values, preferences, and priorities—or our decision to advocate for particular outcomes. As William G. Tierney explains in his essay, "Not all advocacy requires research."

Connecting Research, Advocacy, and Policy

Understanding the orientations that undergird our work is one step toward understanding how we choose to engage in research and advocacy that advances equity, inclusiveness, and social change in higher education. Although I and the others in this volume hope that we are contributing to the advancement of these goals, more work is needed. Drawing on his experience serving as deputy assistant at the US Department of Education and in other roles, James T. Minor offers a sobering critique of the limited contribution of most academic research to higher education policymaking. Adam Gamoran, president of the William T. Grant Foundation, also notes the modest impact of most research. Jeannie Oakes and Anthony A. Berryman observe "how far our profession and society have fallen short" in the past one hundred years of educational research.

Essay authors offer differing perspectives on how to connect research and policy. Reflecting the view that many forces influence whether and how research is used in policymaking processes (Head 2010), Heller urges "scholars who wish to use their work to help influence policy . . . to be patient, persistent, and willing to accept small and infrequent victories." Other authors (e.g., Minor, Chang, Crazy Bull, Harper, Goldrick-Rab, Oakes, and Berryman) express less patience, articulating activities that scholar-activists and public scholars may use to more proactively advance policy change.

The views expressed in the essays differ in other ways, as we might expect, given the freedom of academic researchers to make choices based on individually defined guiding orientations. Together the essays in this volume suggest that academic researchers who seek to advance equity, inclusiveness, and social change in higher education should consider their own answers to each of the following questions:

- Are we engaging in advocacy for proclamation or persuasion?
- What are our relationships with relevant stakeholders?
- How are we communicating the results of our research?
- How are we recognizing our roles and responsibilities?

Advocacy for Proclamation and Persuasion

One way to determine whether and how to distinguish between research and advocacy in our efforts to advance equity, inclusiveness, and social change may be to consider our definition of advocacy. Some social psychologists define advocacy as "an expression of support for, or opposition to, something" (Cheatham and Tormala 2017, 3). Using this definition, all academic researchers are advocates. We choose our research topics, theoretical perspectives, and methodological approaches. These choices reflect our values, preferences, and priorities and, as such, are political acts (Perna 2016; Rhoades 2006).

Other social psychologists offer more nuance, distinguishing between advocacy as proclamation and advocacy as persuasion (Akhtar and Wheeler 2016). Whereas advocacy as proclamation involves standing up for particular views and values, advocacy as persuasion suggests a willingness to exchange different viewpoints, debate or defend the nature of the underlying data and research, and even change a conclusion in light of new data or research. Advocacy as proclamation may or may not be grounded in data or research to support the proclaimed views.

Academic researchers make different choices about when and how to engage in advocacy as proclamation and advocacy as persuasion in different situations and contexts, in both their teaching and their research. Attention to fostering engagement around different viewpoints is particularly important in our roles as teachers. I believe that, rather than shutting down speakers who hold views that conflict with our own (as with the protests against Charles Murray at Middlebury College in March 2017), faculty should encourage dialogue that recognizes different viewpoints. We cannot tolerate racism, bigotry, or social injustice. But, we should teach students to engage critically with the ideas that are being advanced rather than engaging in personal attacks. And we should help students to understand and critique the evidence supporting conclusions, from the perspective of our discipline and areas of expertise.

With regard to research, some academics may choose never to engage in advocacy as proclamation or persuasion, preferring to say nothing publicly and engaging only in the production of research and the dissemination of results to academic audiences. This approach may enable an academic researcher to gain tenure and promotion, but it is unlikely to contribute to advancements in equity, inclusiveness, and social change.

Some stress the importance of grounding advocacy (for proclamation or persuasion) in research-based knowledge. Simon Marginson acknowledges that personal values influence our research agenda and questions, but argues that "we better serve our norms, beliefs, and affinity groups by providing clear, dispassionate social science that tells the world as it is." Similarly, Donald E. Heller reflects that he has "always been cautious to ground [his] advocacy in research." Ann E. Austin notes that "advocacy involves using one's knowledge as a researcher to influence decisions and actions, while also maintaining one's commitment to the use of research-based evidence—not personal preferences or passions—as the basis for the positions and directions one encourages."

Offering another perspective, some authors define themselves as scholar-activists (e.g., Goldrick-Rab) and see advocacy as fundamentally related to their research. Shaun R. Harper is "most devoted to using [his] research and privileged position to advocate justice on behalf of [his] people." Cheryl Crazy Bull believes that "indigenous researchers have a duty to advocate for personal and tribal self-determination." Passionate and deep commitment to improving equity, inclusiveness, and social change can be an important motivator for investing the many hours required to produce high-quality research and persisting through inevitable research challenges.

Research is a tool that should be used to address pressing problems and inform social change. Academic researchers bring important strategic advantages to discussions of how policymakers and practitioners may best advance equity, inclusiveness, and social change in higher education. As academic researchers, our strategic advantages include using high-quality research designs, data, and methods and grounding our research in appropriate theoretical frameworks. As such, our contributions to advancing equity, inclusiveness, and social change are strongest when advocacy is based on research rather than opinion and anecdote (Perna 2016).

One activity that has the potential to compromise our strategic advantage as academic researchers is accepting funding or other sources of support for our research. Receiving external support for research carries many benefits and is often valued in promotion and tenure processes. But scholars must also consider, as Heller writes, that external funding "can call into question whether the work has an explicit or implicit bias at its genesis." Even when funding sources are disclosed, the presence of potential conflicts of interest may raise questions about the credibility of the research (Lipton, Confessore, and Williams 2016; Lipton and Williams 2016). Our credibility may also be compromised when we overstate the conclusions or implications of available research, or fail to recognize, as Ann Austin cautions, that findings may not be transferable to other contexts.

Relationships with Stakeholders

The ways that we connect research, advocacy, and policy depend on how we define our relationships with relevant stakeholders. Some authors emphasize a goal of understanding the nature of the problem and potential policy solutions from the perspective of intended beneficiaries (e.g., Harper, Goldrick-Rab). Oakes and Berryman encourage researchers to shift attention from "conducting research 'about' problems related to education, whereby groups in question frequently become objects of scientific study," to engaging with those groups as "equal partners capable of expressing their democratic subjectivity."

Several authors use their personal experiences and perspectives to provide insights into problems and add credibility to their research. Christine Stanley describes the benefits she sees of her "insider status" as an "immigrant woman of color in academia who has spent a large part of her career in predominantly White institutional spaces." Cheryl Crazy Bull notes that "in an academic environment that didn't appreciate or foster indigenous research, courageous acts took place to bring attention to our research and scholarship."

Other essays describe efforts to advance equity, inclusiveness, and social change by focusing on the knowledge needs of policymakers and practitioners (Heller, Gamoran, Minor). Essay authors describe efforts to produce research that is of use to college administrators (e.g., Bensimon, Solorzano, Stanley), state policymakers (e.g., Heller), and the judicial system (e.g., Chang, Solorzano).

To conduct research that is relevant to the knowledge needs of policymakers and practitioners, academic researchers must engage in conversations with them (Perna 2016). Adrianna Kezar argues that "engagement should be mutual and two-way—not scholars telling practitioners what to do." Heller describes how he has engaged with state policymakers to understand how they "use academic research to help further their missions." Mitchell J. Chang describes his collaboration with attorneys in affirmative action lawsuits. Estela Mara Bensimon notes that partnering with practitioners "poses its own unique challenges" but identifies the benefits of these collaborations for developing and implementing research-based tools and practices that improve racial equity in educational outcomes.

Adam Gamoran emphasizes the importance of developing productive relationships with potential users of research, including policymakers, practitioners, and "intermediary organizations" that connect researchers with policymakers and practitioners. With support from the William T. Grant Foundation, the 2015 ASHE conference included five presidential sessions that shared insights from five year-long collaborations between academic researchers and representatives of organizations that seek to help higher education policymakers and practitioners identify, understand, and apply research-based evidence. The collaborations were designed to advance the production of high-quality research related to inequality in higher education and improve linkages between the creators and users of higher education research. The five collaborating organizations were the Council on Independent Colleges, National Association of Student Financial Aid Administrators (NASFAA), NASFA: Association of International Educators, Pell Institute, and Western Interstate Commission on Higher Education.[1]

As we learned in these collaborations, and as Adam Gamoran discusses in his essay, developing productive relationships with users of research requires first building trust. Producers and users of research must develop shared understandings of the goals and purposes of the relationship. While potentially mutually beneficial, developing and sustaining relationships requires ongoing commitment. In his essay, Adam Gamoran offers suggestions for constructing potentially fruitful partnerships in higher education, with attention to potential topics and funding sources.

Communication of Results

A consistent theme across the essays in this volume is the value of proactively translating, disseminating, and communicating research results beyond traditional academic audiences. As Mitchell Chang succinctly states, "Empirical evidence alone cannot change the course of history."

All of the essays in this volume are authored by senior scholars—individuals who have successfully met the requirements to advance in their positions. While some authors note that they have been committed to public scholarship since the beginning of their careers, several authors (e.g., Austin, Harper, Tierney) recommend that those who wish to be promoted in the academy continue to recognize the standards and expectations for tenure and promotion. While I and others praise contributions to public engagement in the tenure and promotion letters that we write and acknowledge that public engagement should be recognized in these processes, tenure and promotion criteria at many higher education institutions will likely continue to emphasize and primarily reward articles in peer-reviewed journals, books, and other publications in outlets targeted to academics.

As observed by other authors in this volume, writing for any audience takes time, and time is finite—especially for untenured assistant professors. Communicating in outlets that go beyond traditional academic outlets is also not without controversy, as illustrated in one recent debate about whether "serious academics" advance their ideas through social media (Thomason 2016).

Writing for non-academic audiences also requires particular skills. Learning to write to conform to academic publication norms is not easy, but at least a core objective of doctoral study is to socialize students to these norms. Even less common in doctoral studies is training to communicate with non-academic audiences. Oakes and Berryman note that "many scholars are already adept at writing for broad audiences through op-eds, blogs, and other emerging media," and they encourage "future and junior scholars . . . to learn from those already engaged in these activities."

Another approach to developing expertise in communicating with non-academic audiences is collaboration. I learned much about communicating with policymakers and the media through a collaborative research project with Joni Finney, now professor of practice at Penn's Graduate School of Education and formerly vice president at the National Center for Public Policy and Higher Education. Products from our multiyear examination of the relationship between state policy and higher education attainment in five states included not only presentations at academic conferences and a book published by an academic press (Johns Hopkins University Press, Perna and Finney 2014), but also policy briefs and press releases disseminated directly to policymakers, journalists, and other stakeholders in each of our five study states.

As with all aspects of our work, we choose how to spend our time and communicate our research results. What is essential is being cognizant that we are making choices and recognizing the implications of these choices.

Roles and Responsibilities

The scholars included in this volume are advancing equity, inclusiveness, and social change through activities that connect research, advocacy, and policy. As discussed in the essays that follow, we, as academic researchers, may choose when and how we engage in advocacy as proclamation and persuasion, the perspectives we advance, the relationships we develop with stakeholders, the ways that we learn about problems and potential solutions, and the ways we communicate with intended users and beneficiaries of our work.

As academics, we should recognize the roles and responsibilities that come with our positions. William G. Tierney argues that academics, and especially tenured faculty, have an obligation to "ensure that the academy remains a place where the search for truth is paramount." Reflecting on how we, as academic researchers, are advancing "truth" is even more essential in an era of "post-truth" (Marcus 2016; Sullivan 2016) and "fake news" (Herreria 2017).[2]

To ensure that the academy is a place that preserves the "search for truth," I believe that we must recognize that different individuals may reach different conclusions about the nature of a problem and the most appropriate solutions. As Marginson states, "We cannot require our colleagues or our students to agree with what we think if the intellectual space in which we work is to remain both fecund and free." At the same time, in addition to encouraging productive dialogue that recognizes a diversity of perspectives, we also, as Chang discusses, have an obligation to correct "willful ignorance," which he defines as "the tendency to reject and ignore facts that are inconsistent with one's own hardened and narrow outlook."

Like many academic researchers, I believe we have a moral and ethical obligation to use our positions to advance equity, inclusiveness, and social change. While commitment to these goals drives my work, I also argue that the voices of academic researchers are most effective when what they say is grounded in research, as methodologically rigorous, theoretically grounded research is what differentiates us from other advocates (Perna 2016). If we agree that "policymakers and practitioners need more than data-free assertions" (Perna 2016, 332), then we have an obligation to push ourselves and others to understand and articulate how we know what we know, as well as how (and for what reasons) we believe that others' recommendations are flawed.

We also have an obligation to stand up against racism, bigotry, social injustice, and other violations of core principles and values as well as actions that threaten academic freedom and diminish the value of data and research.

Particularly in this deeply polarized political environment, we, as academic researchers and faculty, have an obligation to raise questions about "alternative facts" and data-free assertions and claims. As Trinity College President Patricia McGuire is quoted as saying, "If we academics don't stand for truth, what's the purpose of what we do?" (Jaschik 2017).

While we may offer varying articulations of the connections among research, advocacy, and policy, I and other authors in this volume agree that more work is required to advance equity, inclusiveness, and social change in higher education, and to persuade key stakeholders about the best policies and practices for achieving these goals. I hope that the reflections in this volume are helpful to early career scholars who are beginning to contemplate how they will connect research, advocacy, and policy, as well as to more seasoned scholars who are reflecting on the choices made to date and the choices to be made in the months and years ahead.

NOTES

1. See http://www.ashe.ws/2015wtgrant for more information about the goals of each collaboration and the products produced, as well as video commentary on the collaborations.

2. *Oxford Dictionaries* (n.d.) defines *post-truth* (adjective) as "relating to or denoting circumstances in which objective facts are less influential in shaping public opinion than appeals to emotion and personal belief" (https://en.oxforddictionaries.com/definition/post-truth).

REFERENCES

Akhtar, Omair, and S. Christian Wheeler. 2016. "Belief in the immutability of attitudes both increases and decreases advocacy." *Journal of Personality and Social Psychology* 111 (4): 475–92.

Baum, Sandy, Jennifer Ma, and Kathleen Payea. 2013. *Education pays: The benefits of higher education for individuals and society.* Washington, DC: The College Board.

Cahalan, Margaret, Laura W. Perna, Mika Yamashita, Roman Ruiz, and Khadish Franklin. 2016. "Indicators of higher education equity in the United States: 2016 historical trend report." Washington, DC: The Pell Institute of the Council for Opportunity in Education and the Alliance for Higher Education and Democracy. http://www.pellinstitute.org/publications -Indicators_of_Higher_Education_Equity_in_the_United_States_2016_Historical_Trend _Report.shtml.

Carnevale, Anthony P., and Stephen J. Rose. 2015. "The economy goes to college: The hidden promise of higher education in the post-industrial service economy." Washington, DC: Georgetown University Center of Education and the Workforce.

Carnevale, Anthony P., Nicole Smith, and Jeff Strohl. 2010. "Help wanted: Projections of jobs and education requirements through 2018." Washington, DC: Georgetown University Center of Education and the Workforce.

Cheatham, Lauren B., and Zakary L. Tormala. 2017. "The curvilinear relationship between attitude certainty and attitudinal advocacy." *Personality and Social Psychology Bulletin* 43: 3–16.

Head, Brian W. 2010. "Reconsidering evidence-based policy: Key issues and challenges." *Policy and Society* 29: 77–94.

Herreria, Carla. 2017. "Fox news anchor stands up for CNN and defines 'fake news.'" *Huffington Post*, February 25. http://bit.ly/2mgYyNo.

Jaschik, Scott. 2017. "Speaking out where others wouldn't." *Inside Higher Ed*, February 20. https://www.insidehighered.com/news/2017/02/20/president-trinity-washington-outspoken -criticism-trump-administration-including.

Lipton, Eric, Nicholas Confessore, and Brooke Williams. 2016. "Think tank scholar or corporate consultant? It depends on the day." *New York Times*, August 8. https://www.nytimes .com/2016/08/09/us/politics/think-tank-scholars-corporate-consultants.html.

Lipton, Eric, and Brooke Williams. 2016. "How think tanks amplify corporate America's influence." *New York Times*, August 7. https://www.nytimes.com/2016/08/08/us/politics/think -tanks-research-and-corporate-lobbying.html.

Marcus, Ruth. 2016. "Welcome to the post-truth presidency." *Washington Post*, December 2. http://wapo.st/2vD90Ui.

Perna, Laura W. 2006. "Studying college choice: A proposed conceptual model." In *Higher education: Handbook of theory and research*, vol. 21, edited by John C. Smart, 99–157. New York: Springer.

Perna, Laura W. 2016. "Throwing down the gauntlet: Ten ways to ensure the future of our research." *Review of Higher Education* 39: 319–38.

Perna, Laura W., and Joni Finney. 2014. *The attainment agenda: State policy leadership in higher education*. Baltimore, MD: Johns Hopkins University Press.

Rhoades, Gary. 2006. "The higher education we choose: A question of balance." *Review of Higher Education* 29: 381–404.

"Statement from the Faculty Senate Executive Committee." 2016. *University of Pennsylvania Almanac* 63 (15), November 22. http://www.upenn.edu/almanac/volumes/v63/n15/faculty -statement.html.

Stripling, Jack. 2017. "Trump's wild ride." *Chronicle of Higher Education*, March 3. http://www .chronicle.com/article/Trump-s-Wild-Ride/239387.

Sullivan, Margaret. 2016. "The post-truth world of the Trump administration is scarier than you think." *Washington Post*, December 4. http://wapo.st/2wz3RKa.

Thomason, Andy. 2016. "What is a 'serious academic'? Social-media critique provokes a backlash." *Chronicle of Higher Education*, August 5. http://www.chronicle.com/blogs/ticker/what -is-a-serious-academic-social-media-critique-provokes-a-backlash/113376.

chapter 2

A Day Late and a Dollar Short

The Relevance of Higher Education Research

JAMES T. MINOR

Over the past decade I have gone from being a tenured faculty member in a top-tier higher education program to serving as a senior strategist for academic success in the nation's largest and most diverse four-year system. Along the way, I have also served as deputy assistant secretary at the US Department of Education and program director at a national non-profit. All of my work in some respect has been focused on improving college completion, strengthening institutional capacity to serve students more effectively, and supporting innovation in higher education. My career trajectory has covered the terrain of the tenure and promotion process at a research institution and federal and state policymaking at the highest levels. Along the journey, higher education research, as a commodity, has had high value when counted as a measure of professional productivity and absolutely no value as a resource to inform policymaking.

If the value of higher education research is measured by its usefulness beyond a professional productivity metric and advocacy, then we must consider its ability to influence change and improvement in the field. I consider advocacy a matter of not only position-taking but also policymaking—the formal process of converting social ideals and research into codes and regulations that often govern behavior and the distribution of resources. I leverage my experience in research communities and policymaking environments to facilitate discussion concerning the role higher education research plays in advocacy and policymaking. In my uncle's terms, as a community of researchers, we are "a day late and a dollar short"—a euphemism for being late-arriving and ill-equipped for an occasion, thereby rendering one irrelevant.

My professional work focuses on the business of improving degree completion nationally while addressing persistent equity gaps for low-income
students and those who may be the first in their family to attend college. The
goal to produce a greater number of college graduates is commonly understood to have serious implications for America's economic future, our ability
to meet workforce demands, and the democratic balance of the nation. Right
now, more Americans between the ages of 25 and 64 have some college but no
degree than have a bachelor's degree. The research, policy, and advocacy issues with which I wrestle are wrapped around the fact that the fastest-growing
groups of young people are among the least likely to graduate from high
school and enter college. Low-income students and first-generation students
who make it to college are also the least likely to graduate. It is numerically
impossible for the nation to achieve the goal of producing more postsecondary credentials without significantly improving success rates among poor and
first-generation students. Yet, these individuals and their communities are dis-
enfranchised socially, economically, and politically. We need focused research
and effective advocacy to improve current college completion rates.

Although there are theoretical connections among research, advocacy, and
policymaking, I argue that each is currently practiced in ways that render them
more detached than connected. Being a public intellectual requires a rare
propensity to work in and across fairly distinct professional communities
with different values and dissimilar rhythms. One true measure of being an
effective public intellectual is the extent to which research or advocacy lead
to improved outcomes for students or better performance by the institutions
they attend.

The challenges associated with college completion beg research focused on
factors associated with student success, policies to improve degree productivity nationally, and strategic advocacy efforts at various levels. In addressing the relationships among research, policy, and advocacy, I reframe each
in ways that summon less conventional ideas about how they are related and
how they potentially influence outcomes for students.

Higher Education Research and Relevance

One unavoidable question concerning higher education research is its use
and utility in settings outside the academy. A related but equally important
question concerns the extent to which higher education research, as a body
of work, is positioned to inform advocacy or policymaking. These questions
have both methodological and practical implications. A group of funders

from national foundations recently convened leading scholars to solicit feedback to inform the development of funding priorities. During introductions, the scholars introduced themselves and their research agendas. By time the fifth person stood up, the eyes of funders had glazed over. Each researcher intricately described narrow scholarly interests that could be placed on the margins of what was defined as a national agenda and funding priorities. Not every higher education researcher is detached in this fashion. Yet, relevance in an academic discipline is currently defined by what is important to individual scholars rather than by a connection to major policy issues and is not measured by its utility for policymakers and practitioners making real-time decisions.

One early policymaking lesson as deputy assistant secretary was understanding the considerable influence of think tanks and advocacy organizations compared to researchers on key higher education issues. For instance, when preparing for a vote on an issue such as the reauthorization of the Higher Education Act, the largest and most significant piece of postsecondary legislation, neither policymakers nor their staffers search the annals of academic journals for perspectives or actionable intelligence. A review of individuals scheduled to testify before congressional committees on college affordability, accreditation standards, campus transparency requirements, and financial aid investments does not yield many researchers or representatives from higher education research associations—organizations ostensibly designed to leverage a community of researchers to inform policymaking.

While academic freedom, tenure, and intellectual property are long-standing values in higher education, these hallmarks can also create safeguards for the production of narrowly focused research that is often more attached to individual intellectual interest than to an intention to influence major policy issues. Notwithstanding the inherent tensions between academic traditions and advocacy, some researchers who intend to address major policy issues are confronted with methodological and resource limitations that compromise the generalizability of their work. The essence of public policy is to, in non-rivalrous ways, improve the well-being of the public without offending existing laws (Van Meter and Van Horn 1975). The goal, generally, is not to understand experiential nuances at the individual level but to advance social and educational policies that are good for the masses (Kimbrough 1964; Meranto 1967). These natural tensions between purpose and design often limit the relevance of higher education research in policy environments.

The relevance of higher education research is not only a matter of conceptual compatibility. Relevance also has to do with the timing and placement of research. Even studies that are conceptually and methodically aligned with policy deliberations could be deemed irrelevant if they are not accessible to advocates when they need them. Beyond simply translating higher education research for various audiences, researchers must effectively place research in policy environments for advocates to consider. Strategic placement is different from the academic tradition of archiving, where the final step is publication. Strategic placement requires scholars to be in sync with advocacy and policymaking activities that typically occur outside of academic communities. Placement also requires scholars to actively move their work closer to the center of policy debates, whether at the institutional, state, or federal level. In recent years, states like Texas and Florida have passed state-wide legislation to govern how developmental education is practiced across postsecondary institutions. National non-profits were major advocates for the legislation and played a significant role in shaping it. What most scholars consider as higher education research did not play a role. Advocacy, by definition, is designed to support a cause or a proposed change in policy. In its most modest form, it should responsibly inform decision making.

Rethinking the relevance of higher education research requires an examination of whether too much of what is valued as scholarship is so narrowly focused and imperceptible that it has no utility for policymakers or practitioners working to solve real, present-day problems. The connections among research, advocacy, and policymaking can be strengthened by more intentionally designing scholarly agendas that, from the outset, address actionable and current issues of the day. Research communities and associations must also be able to leverage collective wisdom, resources, and expertise in more purposeful ways that go beyond convening annually.

Ideology as a Moderator

Discussions of the relationships among research, advocacy, and policymaking often ignore a critical moderator: ideology. We often assume that if you provide a group of smart decision makers with credible research about how to make college more affordable, they will produce decision outcomes to that end. This idealized view does not take into account ideological variance among advocates and decision makers. Research, advocacy, and policymaking, in many instances, are reflections of ideology. Research, with all of its ethical provisions, in the best case renders value-neutral findings to be considered. In the worst case, research can be used, ignored, and manipulated to fortify ideological positions. All actors—researchers, advocates, and policymakers—begin with ideological values that color the pursuit, interpretation, and use of research.

Value propositions that consider whether every student, regardless of background, deserves a high-quality education or whether the government should have an interest in ensuring college classrooms are diverse elicit positions based on ideology, not necessarily research. In the same way, decisions about need-based aid versus merit-based aid, the responsibility of taxpayers to support public higher education, and campus discipline policies related to sexual assault are first understood through ideological lenses. Ideas about social justice, equity, fiscal responsibility, race relations in America, and the place of guns in society are often formed independent of research. Very little social science or advocacy is agnostic or pure in the sense that the ideology of the researcher is undetectable. Some argue that social scientists should be value-neutral and that the role of the researcher is to offer unbiased findings to inform understanding of social phenomena. Others argue that it is unreasonable to expect researchers to be ideologically detached from their work and that researchers are inherently advocates.

Scholars study issues about which they care deeply and that give them a sense of purpose, as a way to make a difference while accounting for their biases. The idea that higher education researchers somehow exempt themselves from advocacy is unrealistic. We are constantly advocating for what we believe in—sometimes unknowingly. Scholars advocate in the classes they teach, the textbooks they assign, and the lectures they deliver, as well as in other professional activities. The distinction has to do with the degree to which that advocacy is organized, intentional, and targeted to advance a specific outcome or policy agenda in the absence of research.

There are varying levels of advocacy. An ideological belief in equal opportunity may commit someone to making college affordable for poor students. One person might quietly contribute to a scholarship fund. Another individual, with similar ideological beliefs, might join with students protesting tuition increases. Someone else might organize politically to address the same issue. Any social change—school desegregation, civil rights legislation, or marriage equality, for instance—involves advocacy and activism at multiple levels. David Bornstein, in his book *How to Change the World: Social Entrepreneurs and the Power of New Ideas*, contends, "An idea is like a play. It needs a good producer and a good promoter even if it is a masterpiece. Otherwise the play may never open; or it may open but, for a lack of an audience, close after a week. Similarly, an idea will not move from the fringes to the mainstream simply because it is good; it must be skillfully marketed before it will actually shift people's perceptions and behavior" (2007, 93). The question vexing higher education scholars is not whether they should be considered advocates or public intellectuals, but whether their advocacy, including their research, is organized or effective in ways that are consequential.

Looking Forward

There is one serious indictment of the higher education research community that scholars must take seriously. Right now, innovation and the most influential studies are not attributable to card-carrying research association members in the higher education community. At a recent association meeting, I asked leaders to name the association's two most significant accomplishments in the past three years. Most struggled to identify achievements that mattered outside of the association or to offer examples of how the organization leveraged research or advocacy efforts to bring about significant change. National non-profit organizations, think tanks, and even large consulting outfits with national security contracts in their portfolios represent the most audible voices in higher education policy environments. It could also be argued that the most aggressive and effective advocates for change and innovation in higher education also come from outside the higher education research community. If this is true, then the role and purpose of higher education research must be reexamined communally, assuming research is not conducted simply for the sake of conducting research.

During a recent legislative hearing on higher education innovation, a member of the committee exclaimed that few, if any, industries have been in business for as long as universities, yet know so little about the efficacy of the products and services provided. Right now, roughly 40 percent of students who begin college at four-year institutions graduate four years later. About 60 percent earn degrees six years after enrolling (Synder et al. 2016). While some will quibble with the metrics used to measure college completion rates, the bottom line is too few students who enter college actually earn degrees. At issue is the capacity of the higher education research community to deliver solutions that address what is now described as a national imperative. Although higher education research as an academic discipline has grown tremendously, fundamental questions remain about the effectiveness of long-standing practices and the innovations that are worthy of investment.

There is no question that, as a community, higher education research is a day late and dollar short. The relevance and utility of higher education research is currently misaligned with national advocacy and policy initiatives. The cumulative value of higher education research is not currently organized or positioned to effectively advocate for change in ways that improve the likelihood that more students achieve their postsecondary goals. As a result, debating about whether individual researchers should advocate as a matter of academic or intellectual integrity is futile. The collective impact and relevance of the research community is the much more important question.

REFERENCES

Bornstein, David. 2007. *How to change the world: Social entrepreneurs and the power of new ideas.* New York: Oxford University Press.

Kimbrough, Ralph B. 1964. *Political power and educational decision-making.* Chicago: Rand McNally.

Meranto, Philip J. 1967. *The politics of federal aid to education in 1965: A study in political innovation.* Syracuse, NY: Syracuse University Press.

Synder, Thomas, Cristobal de Brey, and Sally A. Dillow. 2016. *Digest of educational statistics 2015.* Washington, DC: National Center for Education Statistics.

Van Meter, Donald, and Carl Van Horn. 1975. "The policy implementation process: A conceptual framework." *Administration and Society* 6 (4): 445–88.

chapter 3

Changing the Course of History

Imagining New Possibilities for Addressing Old Business

MITCHELL J. CHANG

I am only a few years away from qualifying for early retirement. When I joined the faculty of the University of California at Los Angeles (UCLA) as an assistant professor, I dreamed about exercising this option. I imagined at the time that by retiring early I would still be young enough to continue pursuing my passion: surfing. Since then, my dream of early retirement to devote my days to being in the ocean has been derailed by unforeseen circumstances. First, I did not expect to age out of my beloved sport by middle age. My wetsuits are no longer chronically damp as the physical demands have become exceedingly challenging. Second, I have found myself increasingly more concerned about what I described as "unfinished business" in an article published in the *Journal Committed to Social Change on Race and Ethnicity* (*JCSCORE*; Chang 2015).

In that article, I was invited to advise on the future direction for *JCSCORE*, a new journal seeking to accelerate the transformation of higher education by documenting ways to enhance learning and improve human relations within, across, and through colleges and universities. The editors invited me to do this because I have steadfastly contributed over two decades of research that informs the broad set of topics and issues concerning diversity in higher education. In that *JCSCORE* article, I raised concerns about why the robust exchange of ideas nested within the academic world does not necessarily make a meaningful difference in the real world—or move the course of history toward greater positive "social change." Because my thoughts in that article are relevant to the questions posed by Laura Perna about research and advocacy, I draw from it for this essay.

My thoughts shared here are based less on empirical evidence and more on my gut feeling, which is disturbed by a growing anxiety. As I move into what will likely be the last quarter of my career and as my children become young adults, I have become increasingly more impatient when it comes to social change. I fully expected by now that racial disparities and antipathies would be lessons that my children would read in high school history books rather than in the daily news or on the playground. I'm reminded almost weekly by what I see in mainstream media and experience in life that race relations and racism may not be significantly better today than they were in my childhood. In some pockets of our nation, circumstances may even be getting worse, as illustrated by the unprecedented numbers and intensity of student protests on college campuses in fall 2015.

Perhaps my expectations about the speed of change toward improved learning and human relations across racial and cultural differences by eradicating racism were too ambitious and even implausible. Yet, for an Asian American who emigrated from Taiwan and grew up under the protection of the 1964 Civil Rights Act, those expectations seemed realistic and the setbacks have been especially painful. At certain times, however, even the setbacks have seemed to open a window of opportunity to enact meaningful social change. For example, when I arrived in Los Angeles for graduate studies in 1992 only a few months after riots erupted following the acquittal of the four police officers who assaulted Rodney King, I experienced a shared sense of urgency and responsibility for transforming the meaning and impact of race in U.S. society. Many unexpected turns eventually derailed that collective momentum, and we failed to take care of business.

Looking back on the string of opportunities and setbacks, I don't think that the failure to advance social change and settle a long trail of unfinished business is centrally an intellectual or empirical failure. I know firsthand that scholars and practitioners have established important insights, grounded in rigorous empirical research published across a wide range of high-impact journals. Yet, another generation of youths is stuck in failed schools, neglected neighborhoods, and a cycle of racial crises, leaving them with little hope for the future, despite those significant intellectual gains.

The persistence of the problems we face today suggests that the rich body of scholarship and research that inform race has not yet reached broadly or deeply enough to make a meaningful difference. If so, there are vital yet overlooked problems regarding the application of the already rich body of scholarship. In applying research, countless issues are outside of a researcher's direct control, including negotiating political forces and obtaining adequate resources to launch empirically informed practices. Still, as a community of researchers, we can do more to change the course of history. Toward that interest, I highlight how I try to be intentional about applying my own research, which examines broadly the intersection of racial dynamics and US higher education. By sharing this, I hope to trigger the reader's imagination about the application of research. To the extent that these suggestions go beyond informing policymakers and practitioners, they may also provide insight into advocacy from the position of someone who mainly conducts empirical research.

During my first-year of doctoral studies, I read Thomas Kuhn's (1970) groundbreaking analysis of scientific research. Kuhn observed that, as a body of research advances, the knowledge base necessarily becomes more specialized, and those contributing to it become increasingly more likely to work within a well-defined set of assumptions or "paradigm." This type of knowledge accumulation promotes a tendency in a community of scholars to look inward within itself to build a mountain of empirical evidence, rather than outward to make the knowledge applicable to society. This tendency, according to Stephen Steinberg (2007), can fixate a research community's gaze inwardly onto scholarship for its own sake at the expense of gazing outwardly to solve real-world problems.

While gazing inwardly to advance knowledge in systematic and rigorous ways is extremely important, I now devote just as much attention to gazing outwardly. I do this in two distinct ways. I first try to achieve a solid experiential sense or *ground-level* understanding of the problems I study. I came to appreciate this approach after I completed my master's degree and then went to work for two years for a school district in San José, California, that served an economically challenged and racially diverse area. I thought I was well prepared for the job because I had taken many courses and wrote dozens of term papers that addressed educational inequality. While this academic knowledge base provided a foundational understanding of the problems, I developed a much better sense of how inequality played out on a daily basis while working in the schools. This kind of exposure, although not as extensive, provides a rich understanding of the lives that might potentially be affected by my research and how my scholarship can realistically improve their circumstances.

Another way I intentionally gaze outwardly is to reach beyond educational researchers. I do this by writing in a wide range of publications, including peer-reviewed journals, trade publications, and local newspapers. Writing in different formats and styles enables me to both reach a broader audience and think about the application of my research in different ways. I also work with others outside of my scholarly community to apply research. In the case of my work regarding diversity in higher education, I have collaborated with various teams of lawyers to defend the constitutionality of race-conscious admissions practices and with student affairs practitioners to maximize for students the educational benefits associated with being a member of a diverse student body.

My approach to applying research has also been guided by another book that I read during my doctoral studies: C. Wright Mills's *Sociological Imagination* (1959). Mills argued that to improve the application of research for addressing real-world problems, scholarly communities must invigorate and expand their field's sociological imagination. In other words, empirical research should be guided by a broader vision and purpose. Thus, academic research, according to Mills, should ideally both document what is happening in the real world and provide a vision of a better future world. While the former point is already accounted for in how most of us conduct research, the latter is rarely acknowledged. Embracing a vision of social change encourages us to be more forward-looking and guides the application and organization of research toward a purposeful direction. After all, social change is much more than an empirical project and ultimately requires inspiring, inventing, and sustaining transformative actions.

In imagining social change associated with race in the United States, I often turn to those who blend the science that illuminates racial meaning and structures on the one hand with the art of rearranging meaning and inventing alternative structures on the other hand. Whereas the former is guided by attention to a strict method of inquiry that builds on existing knowledge, the latter is guided by attention to a philosophy of inquiry that broadens existing practices. Cornell West (1993) has provided such guidance for me, but by no means should the aim be to embrace only one way of imagining social change. Historically, we have had the opportunity to examine carefully and to critique vigorously multiple and competing visions that can guide the application of research. Consider, for example, the competing visions between W. E. B. DuBois and Booker T. Washington, and between Martin Luther King and Malcolm X. Each of these visionaries employed his own unique blending of the world of scientific absolutes, applied approximations, and theoretical/philosophical orientation to imagine a pathway to racial justice. At the same time, differences in their unique blends show stark contrasts in how each pursued transformative action.

These visionaries have also shown that empirical evidence alone cannot change the course of history. Even if we imagine promising new forms of social and collective possibilities based on the existing knowledge base, we still must raise consciousness to the point at which the general public will act. Thus, another key to applying research is to establish collaborative networks that provide the general public not only with a more complete picture of social possibilities but also with inspiration to enact that vision.

The media is a powerful collaborator for shaping public consciousness, but here I admittedly have little experience. It seems that popular media outlets can effectively expand our thinking and imagination by challenging tired stereotypes that reduce our capacity to see a wider range of perspectives within a single category and by encouraging us to act with greater compassion toward individuals unlike us. As a fan of television programs that feature great food, I have seen this potential through Anthony Bourdain's *Parts Unknown* and Eddie Huang's *Huang's World*, which challenge narrow views about different groups and the world more generally. Such shows tend to raise our hopes and unite us, more than they fuel our fears and divide us.

Whatever the platform, the application of research is facilitated by addressing willful ignorance—the tendency to reject and ignore facts that are inconsistent with one's own hardened and narrow outlook. Correcting willful ignorance will require intentionally developing new partnerships that can move the public to enter different spheres of knowledge. Harvard professor Henry Louis Gates Jr., who earned a doctorate in English literature, clearly understands the importance of such partnerships and has been engaging in documentary filmmaking and producing and hosting various television series. Unquestionably, Gates's re-imagination of scholarship has broadened the impact of his academic research.

While I have grown increasingly more anxious about the lack of progress as my career winds down, I also fully appreciate that significant gains have been made. My own department at UCLA is a reflection of those gains, as it has become more diverse since I joined the faculty. I was only the second faculty member of Asian descent to be tenured in my department, but now I am no longer the lonely point person for my race. Don Nakanishi, who pioneered the field of Asian American studies, was the first faculty member of Asian descent to be tenured in my department, and he served as my co-advisor with Sandy Astin when I was a student at UCLA.

When Don unexpectedly passed away in March 2016, I was reminded of his extraordinary achievements. One of those was winning a bitter tenure battle at UCLA (Nakanishi 2009). When he fought for tenure in the late 1980s, he knew that it would be a game changer for, in his words, "minority and women scholars who would be reviewed for tenure at UCLA in subsequent years." (198) When my own father heard of Don's case, he discouraged me from pursuing a faculty career, thinking that I too would run into similar opposition. But Don had already paid the heavy price of admission and, subsequently, opened the door wide for me and for those with non-traditional backgrounds and scholarly interests who later joined our department. Upon Don's passing, he was praised for taking risks that pushed the boundaries of scholarship. He was celebrated for his extraordinary courage and commitment to justice, which enabled him to change the course of history not only at UCLA but also across the nation.

If the long-term goal we set for ourselves extends beyond academic contributions toward deeper and broader impact, it will take more than just intellectual engagement. As modeled by Don Nakanishi, we also have to marshal our courage to broaden scholarly impact. In this essay, I have highlighted only a few ways to improve the application of research toward advancing social change, but each in practice will require a heavy dose of courage as they all push traditional boundaries of academic discourse. Working outside the strict format and rules of one's profession can be risky, especially for emerging scholars, as promotion is typically evaluated by what Brian Pusser (2015) argues are norms and assumptions settled by historical agreement. As such, those of us who are established scholars—those who have earned tenure— must deploy our privileges to reconsider what counts as noteworthy scholarship and make room for a wider range of contributions that can advance social change.

I'm quite optimistic that the next generation of scholars will come closer to settling the unfinished business than mine did. When I peek into the social media world of my teenage sons, I notice that they are inventing new relationships and structures that are beyond my imagination. As researchers document and make sense of shifts in the meaning and structure of race, we will need to grapple with the implications of those shifts for social policy, political processes, civic participation, and cultural life. It will be important to draw not only from the existing knowledge base but also from imaginations shaped by lived experiences in unique contexts. By documenting racial dynamics and order as they currently exist and offering new forms of knowing, seeing, and imagining the significance of race, perhaps we, as a scholarly community, can increase the likelihood that future generations of scholars will not have to address our unfinished business. The opportunity to facilitate new possibilities for addressing old business and my declining physical ability to continue chasing waves provide me with two great reasons to forgo early retirement.

REFERENCES

Chang, Mitchell J. 2015. "Applying our imagination to settle unfinished business." *Journal Committed to Social Change on Race and Ethnicity* 1: 5–20.

Kuhn, Thomas S. 1970. *The structure of scientific revolutions.* Chicago: University of Chicago Press.

Mills, C. Wright. 1959. *Sociological imagination.* New York: Oxford University Press.

Nakanishi, Don T. 2009. "Why I fought." *Amerasia* 35: 191–207.

Pusser, Brian. 2015. "A critical approach to power in higher education." In *Critical approaches to the study of higher education: A practical introduction*, edited by Ana M. Martínez-Alemán, Brian Pusser, and Estela Mara Bensimon, 59–79. Baltimore, MD: Johns Hopkins University Press.

Steinberg, Stephen. 2007. *Race relations: A critique.* Stanford, CA: Stanford University Press.

West, Cornell. 1993. *Race matters.* Boston, MA: Beacon Press.

chapter 4

Using Postsecondary Research to Influence the Policy Process

DONALD E. HELLER

Education, as a professional field, has a large body of research that is focused on practical solutions to pressing problems of policy and practice. Because education is such a universal in our society—almost everybody has been a student at one time or is a parent of school students—the media take wide notice of research in the field. Problems in education, and the inquiries that propose to address these problems, are often reported on and dissected by the press.

Higher education, as a subset of education more broadly, is not immune from this scrutiny. While participation in college is not as universal as K–12 schooling, the most current data from the US Department of Education show that approximately 70 percent of high school graduates attend some form of postsecondary education within a year of graduation (National Center for Education Statistics 2016). Thus, research about our nation's colleges and universities often attracts as much attention as that focused on elementary and secondary education.

My own areas of research, which have focused primarily on questions of college access and success for historically underserved populations, have been particularly suited to connection with policy and practice. Upon starting my career, I chose these questions because I found them intellectually interesting and challenging, and I believed they were questions that could address important policy issues. I also discovered as my career moved forward that these were topics that were of great interest to policymakers, the media, policy organizations, foundations, think tanks, and college campuses.

From early on, I was interested not just in conducting research for its own sake and that would be of interest only to other scholars, but in asking questions and providing answers that could influence policy. I had the opportunity in graduate school to train with and be connected to scholars who often bridged the worlds of academia, policy, and practice, so I had mentors who modeled this behavior. It was an easy transition for me to understand how my own work, as it developed, could similarly help have an impact on the real world.

It has also been very satisfying to see how my research has connected with and been able to influence policy and practice. While we would like to think that public policy decisions are driven strongly by academic research, the reality—particularly in the educational arena—is that many important decisions are made without consideration of what the research would recommend. Thus, scholars who wish to use their work to help influence policy have to be patient, persistent, and willing to accept small and infrequent victories.

While I have never labeled myself a "public intellectual," I have taken pride in trying to translate my own research beyond the research and policy communities into a broader realm. This is often done through op-ed or commentary articles (I have published over fifty of these during my career), as well as being available for interviews by journalists and the trade and general press.

Identifying Relevant Topics

As I have often advised my own dissertation students, the best questions are ones about which the researcher can feel great passion. It is generally easiest to motivate yourself if you are interested in the topic and believe it has important significance. One of the advantages that most faculty enjoy is the freedom to pursue questions that interest them, rather than those that are chosen by outsiders. This freedom allows us to choose topics that we find the most interesting, as opposed to those that primarily support the organization in which we work.

At the same time, however, there are practical considerations that most researchers need to consider. First and foremost, while it is important to have an interest in the topics that you are pursuing, it is equally—and some would argue even more—important that the topics be of interest to others as well. It is critical that faculty, especially early in their career as they are working toward tenure, engage in academic communities and take the necessary steps to achieve academic relevance and success. To do so, faculty members must consider how valuable their research will be to journal editors, conference organizers, book publishers, and funders.

In my own research, while I have generally started with questions in which

I have had a strong intellectual interest, and that I believed were of interest to the academic community, I have also considered how important the questions are to others outside of the academy. As I am thinking about a potential research topic, I often ask myself such questions as

- What types of organizations in the worlds of policy and practice may be interested in this research?
- Will this topic be likely to attract the attention of the media? If so, will it be the general press or only specialized publications, that is, those focused on education in general or higher education specifically?
- Will university administrators on my own or other campuses be interested in the study?

Answering these questions is easier if the researcher engages with these constituencies on a regular basis and in a meaningful fashion, and understands how these constituencies use academic research to help further their missions. Ways to do this include the following:

- Attending conferences of non-academic organizations and connecting with individuals in policy and administrative positions.
- Working with your university's news office to identify topics that are of interest to the media and using it to connect you with reporters to discuss these topics.
- Talking with administrators on your own campus (or others) to understand the most pressing questions they face in their work.
- Condensing and summarizing academic research in ways that make it more accessible to lay readers. This can mean boiling a thirty-page journal article down to a one- or two-page research brief couched in much simpler and accessible language.

Informing versus Advocating

In my own work, I have at times considered myself to be an advocate for policies that I believed, based on the research that I and others had conducted, would help to promote more equality of opportunity in postsecondary education. In acting as an advocate, I have always been cautious to ground my advocacy in research, so that I could demonstrate to the organizations with whom I was working—both government agencies and non-governmental organizations—that the positions I was taking were more than my own opinion, but were based on strong, empirical research.

In recent years there has been much attention given to the issue of bias in academic research. While education generally has less funded research than many other fields, particularly in the sciences, concerns have been raised about the influence of non-commercial sponsors in our field and the growing role that these sponsors may play in shaping educational policy debates. For example, Reckhow and Snyder (2014) examined the role of foundations in sponsoring research on education, with attention to whether foundations used their research funding as a mechanism for influencing educational policy debates. Utilizing social network analysis, Reckhow and Snyder examined the connections among these philanthropic foundations, particularly those that were relatively new to education funding. They concluded, "Philanthropists have acted as patrons for new voices in education politics, funding increasing numbers of national advocacy groups. However, the concept of patronage does not fully capture the role of foundations in education policy advocacy. Philanthropic support for jurisdictional challengers suggests strong alignment of funding for research, advocacy, and implementation to advance a policy agenda" (193). The same argument could be made for research funded by other types of organizations, whether they be groups that advocate for certain sectors of education (e.g., charter schools, for-profit colleges, public research universities) or those that represent specific stakeholders in education (e.g., employee unions, service providers).

When these foundations and other organizations fund the research of academic scholars, it can call into question whether the work has an explicit or implicit bias at its genesis. In order to maintain the objectivity of the research, it is critical that academic researchers avoid any perception, whether because of the funding source or for other reasons, that the work is anything less than fully objective.

Having said this, there should be no reason why a rigorous research study conducted by a member of the academy should not be used to influence the policy process. In my experience, policymakers, in the legislative branch of state or federal governments and in executive branch agencies, do not make decisions solely by analyzing the findings of academic research studies. But they do on occasion incorporate research findings into the crafting of policy. One example from my own work can help illustrate this.

The Tennessee Lottery Scholarship Program

In 2002, the state of Tennessee was considering creating a merit-based scholarship program for college students based on the Georgia HOPE scholarship program. Tennessee's goal was to increase college access and postsecondary attainment in the state, which like most of the South, lagged behind that of the rest of the nation.[1] The Tennessee legislature created a task force to study the idea, supported by staff from the Tennessee Higher Education Commission (THEC), the state's postsecondary coordinating board. Other scholars and I were asked by THEC to meet with the task force and share findings from research we had conducted on merit-based scholarships. While I was paid by THEC for my work for the task force, THEC was neutral in its position; it did not hire me to promote one position or another with respect to whether the state should create a merit-based scholarship program.

I had recently co-edited a report on state merit scholarship programs for the Civil Rights Project (CRP) (Heller and Marin 2002). The research conducted by the scholars in this report was largely consistent in the finding that existing state merit scholarships disproportionately excluded poor and racial minority students from participation because of the criteria used in awarding the grants. In addition, THEC provided me with data on the racial and socioeconomic distribution of students by test score and grade-point average (GPA) in the state.

Based on the findings in the CRP report and my analyses of THEC data, I advised the task force that if it modeled its program on Georgia's HOPE program, it would benefit primarily white and wealthier students in the state. Other scholars with whom the task force consulted, including some who had contributed to the CRP report, provided similar advice. The reason for this conclusion was that the academic achievement criteria used for awarding merit scholarships are generally highly correlated with race and socioeconomic status. White, Asian, and wealthier students tend to have higher grades and test scores as compared to African American, Latino, and low-income students. Scholarships awarded using these criteria will thus disproportionately reward students who already have the highest college-going rates. Other researchers and I argued that if the state hoped to increase postsecondary participation and attainment over the long run, then it should focus the scholarship dollars on those students who currently had the lowest levels of participation.

In the end, the task force recommended creation of a lottery-funded scholarship that was modeled largely on the Georgia HOPE scholarships. However, it did recommend one key difference that I believe was largely influenced by the academic research the panel heard. Unlike the Georgia scholarships, which had the same criteria and scholarship amounts for all students, the Tennessee program established levels of award based on high school GPA and ACT scores. Students with lower levels of academic achievement (a high school GPA below 3.0, for example) who would not have qualified for the Georgia program would still receive some funding in the Tennessee model. In addition, students from families with incomes below $36,000 (which at the time was approximately the median income level in the state) would have their scholarships topped-up with an additional $1,000 in grant aid.[2]

I considered this a small but important victory. Counter to what had happened in other states, the Tennessee task force had explicitly reached out to academic researchers in creating the new scholarship program and used their analyses in crafting the new program to help make it more equitable and more likely to help the state reach its goal of increasing postsecondary participation and attainment rates in the state. While the task force did not accept all our recommendations, it implemented enough of them that the program was crafted in a way to better help the state meet its goals.

Postsecondary education research can help influence the worlds of policy and practice. Academic researchers have to ensure that their work is well designed and executed, is free of biases, and can withstand the scrutiny of rigorous peer review. Studies achieving this standard can also withstand the scrutiny that is likely to be heaped upon them when they are brought to the worlds of policy and practice.

University-based researchers should also remember that an academic study will in most cases not make its way on its own into debates among practitioners and policymakers. It is incumbent upon the researchers to seek out opportunities to connect with outside groups and promote their scholarship in ways that make what are often dense, complex, and difficult-to-understand concepts accessible to lay readers. Making the effort to do this takes time and energy, and often will not be rewarded in the promotion and tenure process. But it can very satisfying to see one's work have a real impact on higher education institutions and students.

NOTES

1. Data from the 2000 Census showed that 19.6 percent of Tennessee adults held a bachelor's degree, as compared to 24.4 percent in the nation as a whole. Thirty percent of the 18- to 24-year-old population in the state was enrolled in college in that year, compared to 34 percent across the country (US Census Bureau, 2016).

2. For more on the creation of the Tennessee program, see Ness and Noland (2003) and Heller (2004).

REFERENCES

Heller, Donald E. 2004. "State merit scholarship programs: An overview." In *State merit scholarship programs and racial inequality*, edited by Donald E. Heller and Patricia Marin, 13–22. Cambridge, MA: The Civil Rights Project at Harvard University.

Heller, Donald E., and Patricia Marin (eds.). 2002. *Who should we help? The negative social consequences of merit scholarships*. Cambridge, MA, The Civil Rights Project at Harvard University.

National Center for Education Statistics. 2016. "Table 302.10. Recent high school completers and their enrollment in 2-year and 4-year colleges, by sex: 1960 through 2014." *Digest of Education Statistics*. Washington, DC: US Department of Education. https://nces.ed.gov /programs/digest/d15/tables/dt15_302.10.asp

Ness, Erik, and Brian Noland. 2003. "Tennessee education lottery scholarships: A case study of the policy process." Paper presented at the annual conference of the Association for the Study of Higher Education, Portland, Oregon, November.

Reckhow, Sarah, and Jeffrey W. Snyder. 2014. "The expanding role of philanthropy in education politics." *Educational Researcher* 43: 186–95.

US Census Bureau. 2016. "GCT-P11: Language, school enrollment, and educational attainment: 2000—United States—Congressional district by state; and for Puerto Rico." *American Fact Finder*. Washington, DC: US Census Bureau. http://factfinder.census.gov/faces/table services/jsf/pages/productview.xhtml?pid=DEC_00_SF3_GCTP11.US04PR&prodType =table.

chapter 5

The Activist as Intellectual

SIMON MARGINSON

Before enrolling in a doctoral program, and long before working on global higher education or attending any kind of scholarly conference, I served as the research and policy officer for three collective education organizations in succession. I undertook this work in Australia, while I was between the ages of 24 and 37 years. The organizations were the national unions covering students in higher education, teachers in government schools, and faculty in research universities.

These intensive professional jobs, during which I traveled all over Australia many times but never left its shores, were formative, especially the first four years, when I worked for the national student union. New Left student politics were sophisticated, theorized, communicative, and internationalist, much more so than mainstream Australian party politics. It was a great preparation for what was to come in the more globalized, networked world of the 1990s and after. During those thirteen years, my continuing roles were to educate and inform the union members about the educational policies that affected them and to beef up the evidence-based side of union policy, anchoring our transformative demands in the real world. I learned to develop trails of reasoning that were grounded simultaneously in the possible, the plausible, and the realistic. Those years also entailed many lessons in the tensions between advocacy and investigation and between emotional pulls and dispassionate evidence in public discourse.

After arriving at the teachers' union I soon found that some union leaders had specific ideas about evidence-based policy and that those ideas were different from mine. One day the president of the union, a giant in all respects, told the city of Melbourne on commercial radio that there was a looming oversupply of teachers and that all the teacher-training colleges should be shut down. When the talk-back callers started ringing in to tell him about the teacher shortages at their schools and were then joined by irate union members in the teachers' colleges, he soon realized that, first, he didn't have any evidence; second, he was being severely embarrassed in public; and third, this could happen again. Immediately after the interview, he rang the union's newly appointed neophyte 28-year-old research officer (me) to place an agitated order for evidence that would show that he was right. As I had just finished a report about the teacher shortage, with sixty pages of numbers at the back, that had been tabled in front of the president's nose at the last executive meeting, I knew that his request was trouble. It was not the time to speak truth to power. I got off the phone as quickly as I could and hoped that "Numero Uno" would soon forget. Fortunately, he did.

I was deeply shaken by that call. It was unimaginable that anyone responsible to the members would be indifferent to the actual conditions teachers faced, treat the truth about the education system in which they worked as infinitely malleable, argue that red was blue just to save face, or expect research inquiry to confirm the subterfuge. Student politicians, whatever their ideological predilections, had been more honest. Were adult union leaders just mainstream politicians? It turned out that many of them were. Although certain union leaders evidenced greater integrity, and most of them made profound contributions, over time I became less patient with the evidence-free strategies, normative communications that pressed the same emotional buttons each time, and repetitive internal politics that characterized union work. I also became more curious about the empirical domain and about how education systems worked. I knew that in the collective organizations, we did not have all the answers. We had to deepen our core ideas and knowledge of the world to respond more effectively to the Reagan/Thatcher New Right (as it was called) and open the way to the more empowering and socially responsible society we wanted. I needed to change my work.

I gave up smoking, got married, enrolled in a PhD program, left the education unions, and became faculty. My doctoral study investigated the neoliberal formation of markets in education. It was clear to me why I wanted to work in a university, and I was very fortunate to have the opportunity to fulfill my goal. I wanted to better understand the education policy context in which I had lived for thirteen years in its larger political, economic, cultural, and social settings; contribute to the theorization of these settings; bring the understanding to others via teaching and written scholarship; and thus to contribute to changing policy. The theater of activity changed, but the underlying ideas—agency-centered, egalitarian, internationalist—did not. I retained, and still retain, the social democratic assumptions that underpinned our work in the education unions.

This is part of the answer to the question about the respective demands of research and advocacy. Clearly, if we were pure advocates, we would not be faculty. But we never need to slide into the mentality of the attorney, who uses anything and everything to win the case, to be true to what we are. The core assumptions, the conscious and reflexive values that we hold, our meta-method (Dow 1990), are the secure platform on which we build our intellectual edifices and give meaning to our work. Having anchored our thought in larger matters, we no longer feel the need to guarantee our beliefs, commitments, and constituencies through loaded language or selective evidence—lies, damned lies, and statistics. We better serve our norms, beliefs, and affinity groups by providing clear, dispassionate social science that tells the world as it is. The practice of our core values may evolve over time, as may the issues and arenas in which they are applied, but one of the characteristics of our core values is consistency. That consistency enables us to pursue our values with intellectual honesty while making the best use of the marvelous opportunity that we have to create and share in the creation of potentially powerful knowledge.

To make the best use of the opportunity, those of us who came from the activist side of public life necessarily make one renunciation and one adoption. The renunciation is this: we have to set aside, for ourselves at least, the role of the politician, public administrator, or institutional leader whose task lies at the pivot of relations of power and decision. The politician uses words and knowledge in a different way than faculty researchers do. The difference is irreducible. Faculty researchers can work with the politician and must do so. But to maximize the effectiveness of both politics (or government) and research, there is necessarily a division of labor between them. This division creates a perpetual problem of bridging the gap—the need to make academic work impactful, relevant, and publicly useful. We answer that need by working on topics that are important to many people, communicating our work as well as possible in the public space, and listening to others, not by giving ourselves or selling ourselves to politics and administration or to the market. Client-controlled research provides much more in resources and creates more jobs than genuine scholarly research, but it is usually forgettable to the extent that it becomes public at all. If academic work is collapsed into politics or government, becoming a branch of one or the other, then the particular character that enables academic research to make distinctive and original contributions—its roots in scholarly curiosity and empirical observation—is lost.

That brings me to the adoption that activist faculty must make. All persons who work as researcher-faculty, whether identifying as activist or not, pursue empirical investigation and theoretical inquiry not only because they are powered by underlying values, but also because they are intellectually curious about the world. Without that curiosity, we would not be researchers. For me, intellectual curiosity is continuous, daily, driving my reading in history, political economy, and social-political theory as well as my sociological research in education. We share this curiosity with many researchers with a diverse range of value positions. This curiosity is what we all have in common at conferences (intellectually at least). Thus, intellectual inquiry, research, and scholarship must become ends in themselves—as well as a means of securing the kind of society that we want. And to emphasize the point, the objectives of curiosity-driven intellectual work, on the one hand, and social activism (or the work of government), on the other hand, are irreducibly distinct.

Nevertheless, researchers who retain the normative concerns of activists continually work to join together the two parts of this dyad, the intellectual and the activist, on a tactical basis. How then might we model the relationship between activism and intellectual inquiry in research on higher education? On January 17, 1979, at the Collège de France in Paris, during his 1978–1979 lectures on liberal governmentality, Michel Foucault talked about two kinds of dyadic relationship. On the one hand, there is a dyad in which the two parts are joined by a "dialectical logic" in which the contrary parts are ultimately rendered homogeneous. On the other hand, there is a dyad of disparate qualities that is joined by a "strategic logic." Foucault stated, "A logic of strategy does not stress contradictory terms in a homogeneity that promises their resolution in a unity. The function of strategic logic is to establish possible connections between disparate terms which remain disparate" (2008, 42). This discussion of the structure of relations is helpful, adding to our understanding of the non-linear world we inhabit. The relations between social activism (or the work of government), on the one hand, and intellectual work, on the other hand, are disparate but joined by a strategic logic. This is not a homogenizing or even a symmetrical relationship, and it has to be continually worked on. Our effectiveness in each domain is maximized when we can move freely between them without losing the specificity of both and when we can use each to interrogate the other. We open our cherished assumptions, our meta-method, to critical thought. We must be able to see things that make us uncomfortable or that ordinarily could not appear if our values prevailed. The imperative of the intellectual life is that we are always open to changing our views, even though mostly we do not. At the same time, we bring our values to bear on our intellectual work, defining the agenda of inquiry and feeding the research questions.

The central importance to faculty work of dispassionate intelligence, honest inquiry and exposition, relentlessly critical thinking, and the maintenance of freedom for all strands of thought (except those that excise the freedom of others) has an ethical consequence. It means we must always encourage intellectualism in others, regardless of their views. I have never understood those of our colleagues who assess a journal article or a student essay according to whether it advances their own political philosophy or their favorite discipline or theory. That view can only be adopted if one believes there is only one possible account of truth (Carabelli and Cedrini 2014; Sayer 2000). In the heterogeneous social sciences—and research in higher education studies draws on most social science disciplines at some point—the claim that there is only one possible truth is a very difficult proposition to sustain. There's something satisfying about giving high marks to a brilliant student who sits on the opposite side of the political fence to oneself. It means scholarly values have been upheld and scholarly capacity has been recognized and encouraged. We often choose to work most closely with those who share our view of life, and from there our best ideas may come. However, we cannot require our colleagues or our students to agree with what we think if the intellectual space in which we all work is to remain both fecund and free.

This same coupling of intellectual curiosity and bedrock personal values enters into the teaching function, not only in formal classes but also in works of scholarship and doctoral education. Telling people how the world works, to the extent that we ourselves understand it, is as important as anything we do. Our function above all is not to propagate our own personal thought, to produce the next generation of professors (or administrators or other professionals) as clones of ourselves. Our role is to help students build in themselves the intellectual equipment that enables them to inquire, understand, and create knowledge, and more generally, to form themselves as self-determining beings. To me there has never been any difficulty in reconciling my strongly personal beliefs with a form of teaching that is non-propagandistic and designed to foster the critical intellect as an end in itself. That is because the core of social democracy is self-determining agency (Marginson 2016). The ultimate purpose of faculty research, of the knowledge it makes and the hard and probing questions that it asks, is to broaden the space in which we take command of our fate.

REFERENCES

Carabelli, Anna, and Mario Cedrini. 2014. "Chapter 18 of The General Theory 'further analysed': Economics as a way of thinking." *Cambridge Journal of Economics* 38: 23–47.
Dow, Sheila. 1990. "Beyond dualism." *Cambridge Journal of Economics* 14: 143–57.
Foucault, Michel. 2008. *The birth of biopolitics: Lectures at the Collège de France 1978–1979*, edited by Michel Senellart and translated by Graham Burchell. Houndmills: Palgrave Macmillan.
Marginson, Simon. 2016. *Higher education and the common good.* Melbourne: Melbourne University Publishing.
Sayer, Andrew. 2000. *Realism and social science.* London: Sage.

chapter 6

Researcher as Instrument and Advocate for Inclusive Excellence in Higher Education

CHRISTINE A. STANLEY

There is little disagreement about the fundamental definition of research. Whether you look at a dictionary definition or consider how research is characterized on organizational sites in the private or public sector, you find consistent themes and phraseology: *systematic inquiry, investigation of hypotheses, new interpretations of data, gathering and analysis of information, answering a particular problem, gaining an understanding of underlying reasons, opinions, and motivations,* and so on. There is less agreement on how research should be used to inform policy. Yet, the potential for a strong role for research in higher education reform is particularly important, as underscored in Laura Perna's (2016) call for "throwing down the gauntlet to ensure the future of our research." In this essay, I reflect on my work as a faculty member and senior-level administrator at a public, land-grant, research-intensive, flagship university, which is a member of the Association of American Universities (AAU). I know, beyond a doubt, that I could not have accomplished what I have thus far in my academic and public endeavors without the arsenal of research to advocate for inclusive excellence in higher education.

My research focuses on how faculty advance and develop professionally over the course of their careers. I am especially interested in giving voice to how faculty of color experience predominantly White institutional spaces. My work seeks to understand the reasons, opinions, and motivations that undergird an institution's espoused values, as well as the underlying assumptions, artifacts, and symbols that surround faculty work life. I find this work compelling partly because of my own experiences as an immigrant woman of color in academia who has spent a large part of her career in predominantly

White institutional spaces. I engage in this work because I believe that higher education is key to rectifying many of the social and economic disparities and injustices that plague our society and world. If higher education is our best hope for providing the tools to develop a more equitable world, then it is critical that researchers of higher education pay close attention to how institutions of higher education articulate and enact their diversity and equity goals. I believe that research on the experiences of faculty of color in predominantly White academic institutions is an example of research aimed at the greater public good.

I am aware of the challenges faced by researchers motivated by diversity and social justice goals. But, for those who still caution junior scholars and graduate students of color to steer away from researching phenomena that they care deeply about or who question their objectivity for conducting this research, my response is, "If not us, then who?" Why is a scholar of color's intellectual objectivity called into question when we engage in research related to diversity and social justice? Diversity and social justice research taken up by faculty who reside in marginalized communities brings to the forefront the stark and persistent racial disparities in access, representation, and leadership within higher education, and can expose the resistance from the academic establishment to changing a status quo that has privileged the dominant (White) group. Given the state of affairs in higher education and in our country as a whole, we should be less concerned about those who choose to engage publicly with issues of social justice in higher education and more concerned about those who choose to be silent. The fact that, as a faculty member of color in a predominantly White institution, I am conducting research on the experiences of marginalized groups should bring *more* trustworthiness and credibility to the research, as my insider status can illuminate nuances and empower my research participants to share experiences they may not be comfortable disclosing to members of the dominant group. At the same time, I am fully aware that limitations and biases are part and parcel of being a researcher, and that I am ethically and legally bound by what is required of me as a researcher engaged in human subjects research on sensitive topics.

I conduct research on the experiences of faculty of color in predominantly White institutional spaces in order to effect change in a scholarly community where there is still too much silence around discussions of race and too many examples of "two-faced racism" (Picca and Feagin 2007). Through my research and advocacy, I am committed to getting White colleagues to move from the backstage to the frontstage and openly engage in real, even if difficult, dialogues around diversity and inclusion. My own and others' research on faculty professional development demonstrates that faculty who are made to feel marginalized in academia because of intersections between and among their social and cultural identity characteristics (e.g., age, cultural identity, gender identity or expression, nationality, physical and mental ability, political and ideological perspectives, racial and ethnic identity, religious and spiritual identity, sexual orientation, social and economic status, etc.) experience higher education institutions in multiple, nuanced, and complex ways, as compared to faculty who identify as members of the dominant White majority (Stanley 2006; Tierney 1999). By bringing these varied experiences to light and working to identify and enact structural changes to promote equity, faculty who engage in social justice research, in partnership with university leaders committed to bringing about real change, could be a model for student development, faculty development, and curricular development in colleges and universities. Research on the benefits of having a diverse campus environment is resoundingly clear (e.g., Chang et al. 2006; Gurin et al. 2002; Hurtado et al. 1997; Milem 2003; Olivas 1986, 2009; Smith and Schonfeld 2000; Turner, Gonzalez, and Wood 2008). My ultimate goal is for higher education institutions, as Daryl Smith (2015) argues, to live up to diversity's promise for higher education.

My personal experiences on the path that led me to become a tenured full professor and the vice president and associate provost for diversity have significantly influenced my understanding of the connections between research and advocacy. In working with faculty, staff, administrators, and student leaders, I constantly seek to be an advocate for change for the public good, whether that involves decisions that affect personnel processes, procedures, or policymaking on campus. Examples of issues for which I have brought research to bear include access to education, college affordability, campus climate assessment, educational development efforts, pay and other forms of equity, interactions with internal and external university stakeholder groups, faculty recruitment and retention plans, faculty rewards, tenure and promotion guidelines and procedures, leadership succession planning, and university-level strategic plans. In all my discussions in these arenas, I use research to advocate for change. In many instances, the research is the driver of change.

I do not see a distinction between using research to *advocate* for change and using it to *inform* change. In my view, using research to *advocate* for particular reforms in diversity and inclusion is synonymous to using it to *inform* higher education policymakers and practitioners. These words lie along a continuum and are used interchangeably. For example, advocating for a particular reform in my department, college, or university may require using research to speak up and out, to defend or champion an individual or issue, in order to influence a specific, consequential decision. An illustration of this is the decision making that occurs during the review of tenure and promotion dossiers. In this context, advocacy may take the form of bringing to the committee's attention research on implicit bias in the evaluation and promotion of faculty, or research on the impact of the social construction of junior faculty of color as "strugglers" (Fryberg 2010). Advocacy may also take the form of providing narratives that counter narrow, reductionist models of academic excellence and impact that are based on a system that was designed to reward and sustain a master narrative (Stanley 2007).

Similarly, when I think about research as *informing* higher education policymakers and practitioners, it may require providing needed factual information to educate particular groups (e.g., state legislators) about what faculty are doing at the university and about their research's broader benefits to the university's educational mission and to society at large. I may also be advocating for a particular reform. A prime example of the latter is the amicus brief evidence gathered for the *Fisher v. University of Texas at Austin* case taken up by the United States Supreme Court. On June 23, 2016, the Court ruled to reject a challenge to the race-conscious admissions program used at the University of Texas. Justice Anthony Kennedy stated that the admissions program at the university is constitutional based on the university's ability to show that it had narrowly tailored the program to suit its compelling interest of providing its students with the educational benefits of a diverse student body. This ruling could not have occurred without advocacy and informed data. In fact, higher education scholars provided this research evidence years ago (e.g., Chang et al. 2006; Gurin et al. 2002; Milem 2003; Smith 2000) for similar cases brought against the University of Michigan (e.g., *Gratz v. Bollinger* and *Grutter v. Bollinger*). Court cases such as these remind us that we still live in a society where inclusive excellence is not fully realized and evidence-based research is necessary to inform arguments and defend against lawsuits that threaten institutional and stakeholder goals to reflect the social and cultural demographics of the people in our state and nation.

Of specific relevance is the role of professional organizations in advocating for and modeling exclusive excellence, particularly when it comes to working toward the goal of higher education as an equalizer of opportunity. Being a researcher and an advocate for inclusive excellence is challenging and comes with personal and professional consequences that range anywhere from being lauded as a champion to being the canary in a coal mine. The Professional and Organizational Development (POD) Network in Higher Education signaled the validation of my scholarly and advocacy work over the course of twenty-five years when it launched the inaugural Christine A. Stanley Award for Diversity and Inclusion Research in Educational Development in 2016. The award seeks to (1) raise the awareness of and advance theory about diversity issues in educational development, (2) contribute to increased understanding of best practices on diversity-related issues in educational development, and (3) model POD's values of diversity and inclusion in the everyday practice of educational development. I am excited by the prospect for change that the existence of awards like this enables. Professional societies can play a uniquely influential role in advocating for change by giving professional recognition to research efforts by advocates for change.

The researcher as instrument and advocate for inclusive excellence should be synonymous with research that is high quality, has undergone member checking, and is used for organizational accountability efforts. Members of the scholarly community who are underrepresented look to our primary organizational affiliations (e.g., the Association for the Study of Higher Education [ASHE] and the American Educational Research Association [AERA]) to use research to advocate for and model inclusive excellence. I fully embrace the *ASHE Principles of Ethical Conduct* (ASHE 2003) and the responsibilities that come with these principles as a member and researcher. But how do we hold ourselves accountable for inclusive excellence? And how do we ensure that our organizational principles and behavior foster inclusive excellence? The scholarly work of organizational members can and does play a critical role in advancing the discourse to further the work of both organizational and professional interests. For example, scholarship conducted by higher education scholars (e.g., Antonio et al. 2004; Bensimon 2004; Chang 1999; Clayton-Pedersen and McTighe Musil 2009; Hurtado 1992, 2007; Milem, Chang, and Antonio 2005; Pasque et al. 2013; Smith 2015; Turner et al. 2008) was instrumental in resourcing and drafting the National Association of Diversity Officers in Higher Education's Standards of Professional Practice for Chief Diversity Officers, published in the *Journal of Diversity in Higher Education* (Worthington, Stanley, and Lewis 2014).

In my mental model, systematic inquiry and investigation of phenomena is inherently an intellectual endeavor. But, to be more effective, this endeavor needs to be communicated to a broader audience. A public intellectual is someone who has expertise in a particular field of study and communicates that expertise not only through academic outlets, but also to the general public. An example of a public intellectual I admire is the late poet Maya Angelou. The concluding chapter in the book *Maya Angelou: Adventurous Spirit* is titled "Maya Angelou as Public Intellectual" (Wagner-Martin 2015). A recipient of many national and international honors, including the first lifetime Reynolds Professorship of American Studies at Wake Forest University, Maya Angelou used her personal experience and scholarly work to critique interlocking systems of oppression and advocate for dismantling them. Her works have been used to influence, for example, teacher education, race relations, identity development, and community building, and to supplement scientific theory and research in the teaching of child development topics involving self-concept, self-esteem, ego resilience, effects of abuse, parenting, and cognitive development.

When I reflect on public intellectuals, and on Maya Angelou as the epitome of one, and consider my role and responsibilities as researcher-as-instrument, I see an obligation to enter the public sphere. Yet I decide when and to whom I write and speak for the public. I do not respond to every request that comes my way. My strategy is to consider first, who is asking; second, where the connections are to my research expertise; and third, the possible consequences of my decision to accept or not. When I accept an invitation to speak or write, I am regarded on a level that could have the potential to influence decision making or change because my words are backed up by a body of knowledge. I am careful about what I convey and how I convey this knowledge to the public, separating what is opinion from what is based on evidence. My overarching philosophy about responding to these requests, particularly those coming through social media, is to ensure that I am being asked because of what I have to offer based on evidence, rather than opinion. I also know that when I write or speak for the public from my lens of expertise about inclusive excellence, I am the face of a public intellectual. When I speak and write about inclusive excellence in higher education and how it relates to issues of access, affordability, success, institutional values and mission, recruitment and retention, organizational behavior and culture, and social and political forces, I am the face of a public intellectual. The role of a public intellectual is fluid, because the boundaries are not always well defined, particularly so when it comes to social media and its sometimes pernicious impact. I have made a personal decision not to use social media.

In closing, I would go so far as to say that there is a moral obligation to use research for the greater good. Whether we are the instrument or not, research is a process to create new knowledge for the benefit of humanity. As Maya Angelou (1993) said, "History, despite its wrenching pain, cannot be unlived, but if faced with courage, need not be lived again." Advocacy for inclusive excellence in higher education that is based solely on opinion and not on research is easily discounted as merely anecdotal and not given weight in decision making and policy reform. We must not lose sight of making connections to research where possible. This is why I invest my time and energy into the research that I do. I want to break the silence. Inclusive excellence in higher education is determined by how well institutions model their values and engage the richness found among their faculty, staff, and students. We must be courageous instruments, particularly when the challenge that remains for many higher education institutions is to *be the equalizer* and to live up to their espoused values and rhetoric to prepare citizens for an increasingly complex and globalized world in an unknown future.

REFERENCES

Angelou, Maya. 1993. *On the pulse of morning.* New York: Random House.

Antonio, Anthony Lising, Mitchell J. Chang, Kenji Hakuta, David A. Kenny, Shana Levin, and Jeffrey F. Milem. 2004. "Effects of racial diversity on complex thinking in college students." *Psychological Science* 15: 507–10.

Association for the Study of Higher Education. 2003. *ASHE principles of ethical conduct.* Las Vegas, NV: Author.

Bensimon, Estela Mara. 2004. "The diversity scorecard: A learning approach to institutional change." *Change: The Magazine of Higher Learning* 36 (1): 44–52.

Chang, Mitchell J. 1999. "Does racial diversity matter?: The educational impact of a racially diverse undergraduate population." *Journal of College Student Development* 40: 377–95.

Chang, Mitchell J., Nida Denson, Victor Saenz, and Kimberly Misa. 2006. "The educational benefits of sustaining cross-racial interaction among undergraduates." *Journal of Higher Education* 77: 430–55.

Clayton-Pedersen, Alma R., and Caryn McTighe Musil. 2009. "Making excellence inclusive: A framework for embedding diversity and inclusion into colleges and universities' academic excellence mission." Washington, DC: Association of American Colleges and Universities.

Fryberg, Stephanie A. 2010. "Constructing junior faculty of color as strugglers." In *The future of diversity: Academic leaders reflect on American higher education,* edited by Daniel Little and Satya P. Mohanty, 181–218. New York: MacMillan Press.

Gurin, Patricia, Eric Dey, Sylvia Hurtado, and Gerald Gurin. 2002. "Diversity and higher education: Theory and impact on educational outcomes." *Harvard Educational Review* 72: 330–67.

Hurtado, Sylvia. 1992. "The campus racial climate: Contexts of conflict." *Journal of Higher Education* 63: 539–69.

Hurtado, Sylvia. 2007. "Linking diversity with the educational and civic missions of higher education." *Review of Higher Education* 30: 185–96.

Hurtado, Sylvia, Karen Kurotsuchi Inkelas, Charlotte Briggs, and Byung-Shik Rhee. 1997. "Differences in college access and choice among racial/ethnic groups: Identifying continuing barriers." *Research in Higher Education* 38: 43–75.

Milem, Jeffrey F. 2003. "The educational benefits of diversity: Evidence from multiple sectors." In *Compelling interest: Examining the evidence on racial dynamics in higher education*, edited by Mitchell Chang et al., 126–69. Stanford, CA: Stanford University Press.

Milem, Jeffrey F., Mitchell J. Chang, and Anthony Lising Antonio. 2005. *Making diversity work on campus: A research-based perspective*. Washington, DC: Association of American Colleges and Universities.

Olivas, Michael A. 1986. *Latino college students*. New York: Teachers College Press.

Olivas, Michael A. 2009. "Undocumented college students, taxation, and financial aid: A technical note." *Review of Higher Education* 32: 407–16.

Pasque, Penny A., Mark A. Chesler, Jessica Charbeneau, and Corissa Carlson. 2013. "Pedagogical approaches to student racial conflict in the classroom." *Journal of Diversity in Higher Education* 6 (1): 1.

Perna, Laura W. 2016. "Throwing down the gauntlet: Ten ways to ensure the future of our research." *Review of Higher Education* 39: 319–38.

Picca, Leslie H., and Joe R. Feagin. 2007. *Two-faced racism: Whites in the backstage and frontstage*. New York: Routledge.

Smith, Daryl G. 2015. *Diversity's promise for higher education: Making it work*. Baltimore, MD: Johns Hopkins University Press.

Smith, Daryl G., and Natalie B. Schonfeld. 2000. "The benefits of diversity: What the research tells us." *About Campus* 5 (5): 16–23.

Stanley, Christine A. 2006. "Coloring the academic landscape: Faculty of color breaking the silence in predominantly white colleges and universities." *American Educational Research Journal* 43: 701–36.

Stanley, Christine A. 2007. "When counter narratives meet master narratives in the journal editorial-review process." *Educational Researcher* 36: 14–24.

Tierney, William G. 1999. "Models of minority college-going and retention: Cultural integrity versus cultural suicide." *Journal of Negro Education* 68: 80–91.

Turner, Caroline Sotello Viernes, Juan Carlos Gonzalez, and J. Luke Wood. 2008. "Faculty of color in academe." *Journal of Diversity in Higher Education* 1: 139–68.

Wagner-Martin, Linda. 2015. *Maya Angelou: Adventurous spirit*. New York: Bloomsbury.

Worthington, Roger L., Christine A. Stanley, and William T. Lewis, Sr. 2014. "National Association of Diversity Officers in Higher Education Standards of Professional Practice for Chief Diversity Officers." *Journal of Diversity in Higher Education* 7: 227.

chapter 7

Commitment to a Scholarly Life of Contribution, Meaning, and Satisfaction

Engaged Scholarship as Research, Translation, and Advocacy

ANN E. AUSTIN

As a scholar of higher education, I have been committed for many years to doing research that makes a difference in important problems in education and that contributes to a better, more equitable world. I care about the importance of the questions I address and the relevance and power of the methods I use. I care equally about the process of translating research findings into forms that are accessible and useful to those who can use the research. I also care about advocating, informed by research evidence, for policies, programs, and practices that can increase the impact of higher education institutions in fulfilling their missions and contributing to a more equitable and just society. I label myself as an "engaged scholar." Within that label, I include the activities of researching, translating, and advocating.

For twenty-five years, I have been a faculty member at Michigan State University, widely recognized as one of the two oldest land-grant universities in the United States. A commitment to engagement with the challenges and problems of the world is intricately woven into the institutional mission to discover knowledge through research, advance knowledge through teaching, and apply knowledge through service. I am inspired by one of the descriptive slogans of the university—"advancing knowledge, transforming lives"—as it holds up a vision of the scholar as one whose work is based on the discovery and advancement of knowledge for the purposes of improving individual and societal well-being. Guided by this vision, I see my work as an engaged scholar to be defined by a commitment to doing research—that is, framing questions of importance and seeking to understand the answers to those questions through the highest quality, systematic research of which I am capable. I also see my work as an engaged scholar to involve translating what I learn through my research into forms accessible and worthwhile to others in their lives and work. Additionally, I believe being an engaged scholar involves advocacy—defined for me as using the results of the research that I have done, as well as my knowledge of related research, to go beyond only disseminating what I have learned to also using that knowledge to advance a greater good for individuals and society. That is, I am committed as an engaged scholar to participating in deliberations, contributing to and influencing decisions, and helping to frame practical paths of action relevant to the areas in which I have expertise.

As a researcher, I seek to be guided in reaching conclusions and understandings by my best efforts to secure, analyze, and interpret relevant and convincing evidence. As a translator, I believe I must be committed to honesty, perceptiveness, and practicality. I must be honest in explaining findings, and I must be perceptive and practical in determining the ways to present what I have learned so others can understand and use the research. As an advocate, I have a responsibility to use what I know from research to make a difference, or in the words of my university's history and traditions, to use knowledge to "transform lives."

While being an excellent researcher has various challenges, in this essay I focus on exploring the roles of translator and advocate within the responsibilities of an engaged scholar. Two issues involved in translating include recognizing appropriate opportunities for highlighting research findings and developing communication skills that can create bridges from the complexity of research to the questions and interests of a wide array of audiences. I offer three examples of my work as a translator, followed by observations of what I have learned about some of the challenges of translation as scholarly work.

First, during my twenty-five years as a faculty member at my university, I have made myself available to the provost's office and to colleges and departments to consult as well as serve on and lead committees and task forces where my research knowledge can inform institutional policy. Given my research on issues concerning faculty careers and academic work, I have gathered, highlighted, and brought to the attention of institutional leaders research relevant to faculty careers, work/life issues, and strategies to advance women and faculty of color and create more inclusive environments. I see an important part of my role to be a voice—a translator—who introduces relevant research that can inform and frame discussions leading to evidence-based institutional initiatives and policy decisions on issues important to higher education's missions.

Second, I also have served, for about fifteen years, as co-founder and co-principal investigator (PI) / co-leader of the Center for the Integration of Research, Teaching, and Learning (CIRTL), a collaboration of forty-two universities preparing doctoral students to be effective teachers as well as excellent researchers. The preparation of doctoral students who are familiar with the research on teaching and learning and know how to engage in research on their students' learning is a lever for change that affects the larger goal of reforming teaching and learning to ensure the success of a wide diversity of students. My role has involved introducing research about teaching and learning, academic careers, and organizational change processes to colleagues in the science, technology, engineering, and mathematics (STEM) fields, leading research and evaluation efforts about the process and impact of CIRTL's work, and participating as a co-leader of the project in making decisions informed by research.

Third, in addition to serving as a translator at my institution and in a national center, I have recently had the privilege of serving as a program director for almost two years at the National Science Foundation, while on leave from my university. I was invited to this role because of my research on faculty work, reform in STEM education, and organizational change processes. My responsibilities involved translating—that is, bringing to the attention of funding agency leaders and policymakers—research about how higher education reform occurs, what to look for in potential projects aspiring to advance curriculum and teaching reform, and what barriers might undermine reform efforts to strengthen STEM undergraduate education.

In each of these roles, within my university, a national center, and a federal agency, my role as an engaged scholar doing translation work has meant helping decision makers become familiar with research that can be used to inform their thinking. The responsibility and challenges that I have experienced as an engaged scholar are to stay current with related research, perceive strategic moments when inserting related research findings into conversations and meetings would be welcomed and effective, and find ways to do so that are sufficiently relevant, succinct, and collegial in tone that the information is well received. These efforts require appreciating the complexity of the research while also being able and willing to explain it in brief understandable ways that are compelling and useful to those whose work requires moving forward with decisions.

A related issue in terms of the communication process is the avenue through which the communication will occur. An engaged scholar involved in translating the implications of research to a variety of audiences must be willing to present work in a range of venues as well as in traditional peer-reviewed journals—and to develop the skills to write in ways appropriate for those venues. For example, to foster research-based institutional change toward more inclusive environments, a colleague and I have chosen to share our research in the form of a toolkit available through a website (Laursen and Austin 2014), as well as in traditional scholarly venues. I also have had experience in presenting my research as part of a team examining conditions and challenges in higher education in Southeast Asia in the form of a policy monograph for the Asian Development Bank (Asian Development Bank 2011). This form of policy writing is different from typical scholarly writing in peer-reviewed journals. It requires moving from details to patterns, finding compelling examples that illustrate major points while also speaking to multinational audiences, and being able to frame large-scale policy recommendations while also recognizing the particularities of specific contexts. Of course, some scholars also have developed skills in using social media as an avenue for translation.

In addition to research and translation, I see advocacy as part of the work of an engaged scholar. Advocacy goes further than translation in terms of the commitment and direct involvement of the scholar in using research to make a difference in the world. Advocacy goes beyond providing information in accessible forms that can shed light on decision making and activities. Advocacy involves using one's knowledge as a researcher to influence decisions and actions, while also maintaining one's commitment to the use of research-based evidence—not personal preferences or passions—as the basis for the positions and directions one encourages.

Research needs to inform and guide any advocacy I offer, as illustrated in the following example. One of my research projects has focused on studying change strategies used by twenty-five universities committed to creating more inclusive environments, with a particular focus on gender equity in the STEM (science, technology, engineering, and mathematics) fields. The colleague and I who conducted this extensive funded research study are recognized, particularly among leaders at a large group of institutions that have received National Science Foundation ADVANCE Institutional Transformation grants to foster gender equity, as advocates for change in higher education toward more inclusiveness and equity. Often we are pushed by institutional leaders to list "the key three or four interventions an institution should im-plement." Although our roles as engaged scholars involve advocacy for ad-vancing gender equity, and although it is challenging to be pushed by insti-tutional leaders to offer a formula for action, we have resisted taking a facile approach to answering this question. As researchers, we are committed to ensuring that any efforts we make to offer advice to institutions about gender equity are situated not in expediency or personal positions, but in research. One of our research findings is that context matters in selecting interven-tions. Thus, in advocating for change to foster more inclusive campuses, the research findings compel us to recommend careful local study and analysis in preparation for change planning, rather than quick implementation of commonly used strategies.

I provide another example of advocacy as part of the work of an engaged scholar. In 1998, four years after the official end of apartheid, I spent a year as a Fulbright Fellow in South Africa at what is now Nelson Mandela University. Having researched and published on faculty careers, faculty professional development, the experiences of new faculty, and organizational culture and change in higher education, I was asked to work with senior colleagues at the university to design and implement a comprehensive faculty development program that would support faculty as they engaged in rapid organizational transformation and implemented changes in curriculum, teaching, and learn-ing practices designed to be more reflective and inclusive of the diverse South African population. Drawing on extensive research, I helped design a faculty development program that taught academic staff about the research on active learning, including how to create inclusive and supportive classrooms and address the learning needs of a wide diversity of students. While some faculty members were enthusiastic to try research-based teaching strategies, we soon learned that some students were quite resistant to the active learning strate-gies being introduced. They emphasized that they had paid valuable money to be taught—and, from their perspectives, active learning strategies meant the teacher was not doing the teaching. Furthermore, the long-standing assump-tions and behaviors enforced by the previous apartheid system thwarted easy interaction among students from different races and cultural traditions. What became clear was that advocacy of a teaching approach, even when research evidence supported the value of that approach, had to be coupled with keen awareness of cultural conditions (in this case, the educational norms in pre-apartheid South Africa that had defined the previous educational experiences and thus the expectations of many of the students). We needed to prepare students to be participants in classrooms organized around active learning. The lesson was that advocacy as part of the work of an engaged scholar requires attention to context.

I have learned several lessons about advocacy. I believe that an engaged scholar conducts research, translates findings in ways that make sense to the intended audience, and makes decisions to engage in advocacy only when informed by research-based evidence. Advocating without the benefit of thorough and thoughtfully conducted research would diminish the role of the scholar and would violate what I believe are scholars' ethical responsibilities to base their views and their actions on the best research possible. Furthermore, the privilege of providing ideas and input about policy and practice carries with it the responsibility to make public and transparent the research findings supporting those ideas. When I am offering advice, guidance, or input pertaining to policy and practice, my responsibility as a scholar is to explain what research supports my advocacy of particular ideas and why and how the relevant research findings are applicable to the situation. In advocating for ways to nurture more inclusive academic workplaces, for example, my colleague and I explain the research findings that support our recommendations. We are advocates of systemic approaches to change, but we also are committed to providing full information that will enable institutional leaders to make their own decisions based on available data. Similarly, in my work on faculty issues in Asia, the monograph I wrote provided a thorough analysis of data as preface and justification for the policy recommendations offered.

I also believe that advocating for particular recommendations, decisions, or directions should involve explicit attention to the particularity of context. Because one has conducted research in one context does not mean the results are automatically appropriate and relevant in another. While I have encouraged teaching approaches that involve active learning in my work in South Africa, I also have been very alert to consider ways in which findings based on research in western contexts may be inappropriate or limited in the South African context. I also have engaged South African colleagues as collaborators in assessing the relevance of the research findings on which I am basing my guidance and advocacy, encouraging them to make adjustments to the ways in which these research findings might be applied and urging them to conduct their own context-specific research to inform their practices. I also believe that, in engaging in advocacy, an engaged scholar has the responsibility to remember her role as a researcher. Linking research findings to problems of practice in higher education or the broader society leads to new research questions. I have a responsibility to be alert to questions raised by the application of research findings to policy and practice. These questions may lead to further research.

My understanding of my work as an engaged scholar involves the multiple facets of conducting research, translating research findings into forms that are meaningful to relevant audiences, and advocating for programs, policies, and practices for which I believe there is compelling, supportive, research-based evidence. Each of these forms of engaged scholarly work involves rewards, expectations, criteria of excellence, and challenges. I have been rewarded with a sense of meaning and satisfaction as I engage in this kind of scholarship, and I hope my efforts have made a modest contribution in positive ways to the quality of our higher education institutions, our communities, and the lives of others.

REFERENCES

Asian Development Bank. 2011. *Improving instructional quality: Focus on faculty development.* Higher Education in Dynamic Asia Monograph Series. Mandaluyong City, Philippines: Asian Development Bank.

Laursen, Sandra. L., and Ann E. Austin. 2014. *StratEGIC toolkit: Strategies for effecting gender equity and institutional change.* Boulder: University of Colorado. www.strategictoolkit.org.

chapter 8

Choosing How, Why, and to Whom We Profess

Negotiating Professional Neutrality in Public Scholarship

GARY RHOADES

I came into the academy to change it. However, my initial entry into public scholarship was an invitation from an academic union staffer who had read an academic article of mine on retrenchment provisions in collective bargaining agreements (CBAs). So began an ongoing academic life of navigating between the norms and forms of professional neutrality in my scholarly work and those of public scholarship, of speaking and writing that reaches out to public, powerful, and activist audiences for a political purpose. That negotiation involves thinking through choices about audience (to whom we profess), roles and responsibilities as an academic (how we profess), and the purposes of our public performance (why we profess). Professional, ethical, and political considerations surround those choices.

One matter to negotiate is the terms of engagement. In my initial invitation from Christine Maitland of the National Education Association (NEA) I was offered access to a searchable national database the NEA had developed of 211 faculty CBAs negotiated by locals of various unions. Access to this resource was a welcome change from scrolling through library microfiche of limited numbers of contracts. There were two conditions; neither restricted my freedom to frame and publish my analyses—key professional and ethical considerations. First, for a modest stipend I would write a chapter for the *NEA Higher Education Almanac* analyzing a contractual issue of my choice. Second, I would present my findings to faculty leaders and staff at the NEA's annual higher education conference.

For me, this was a win-win-win. This arrangement would enhance my ability to pursue my scholarship on the restructuring of academic labor and institutions. I could observe practitioners involved in the phenomena I was studying, informing my scholarship. Moreover, it offered a creative challenge to engage audiences beyond those in my academic field. I could refine my crafts of writing and speaking. Finally, it spoke to my purpose: connecting my work to groups seeking progressive change in higher education. It fit with my scholarly understanding and lived experience that fundamental change takes place through collective action, often by groups not in formal positions of much power.

Professionally, there were likely costs. Empirically and analytically, my scholarship was outside the mainstream. It did not fit within conventional areas of research in my field on organizations and professions. Moreover, most scholarship was and is oriented to informing managers or powerful policymakers and policymaking bodies. Some would see me as losing objectivity and aligning myself with advocacy groups. This criticism is ironic, given the field's angst about research not being read by leaders and policymakers. That objection constitutes an alignment with established systems and powers that are, to speak their language, addressing issues from their perspective and in their interests.

Such career considerations are, for many, a source of self-censorship, with their own generally unconsidered costs, as status anxieties influence choices about what (not) to study. For me, that would be a Faustian bargain. One reason for being an academic is having the freedom to research and teach what one thinks is important. Another, as part of a social compact with society, is having the opportunity to contribute to a larger purpose of helping the academy and society come closer to fulfilling their expressed ideals. That is why I accepted the NEA's offer.

Over time, my scholarship on unionized faculty and my NEA conference presentations led to other invitations to speak at national, state, and local venues for academic labor groups. Such events extended my opportunity to learn from practitioners, refine my craft as a communicator, and further my purpose of informing social change. And they did so without compromising my academic work's integrity. Indeed, they enhanced it by affording me insight into the back stories behind the negotiations and implementations of the contracts I was analyzing.

In this capacity, I was an independent scholar–expert and researcher. I informed faculty leaders and union staff about developments nationally, and they informed my research about developments locally. For instance, an invitation from Susan Meisenhelder of the California Faculty Association (CFA), one of the nation's largest faculty locals, stemmed from her sense that it would be useful for CFA leaders, who were embedded in their local/state struggles, to see national patterns in restructuring and contractual provisions. Reciprocally, I learned about those struggles from them.

Speaking from such a stance involves a rhetorical and ethical dance. I am a scholar speaking to academics who are not scholars in my field. I am an independent expert from a non-unionized setting speaking to unionized faculty. I sit in my office studying CBAs, whereas the audience members sit at the bargaining table across from management and negotiate (and implement) CBAs. There can be a professional arrogance and ethical isolation from the world we study in the conventional ethos of standing above it all as a politically neutral professional.

That construction of professionalism is classed, raced, and gendered (e.g., Rhoades et al., 2008; Keller 1985). The role of detached expert is professionally, ethically, and politically problematic, as well as empirically inaccurate. It affects who is advantaged in getting into and operating within this culturally specific set of academic norms. It also has implications for what social groups and professional, political, and economic structures are being most served.

In my public scholarship, my credibility lies in being a scholar. But it also lies in connecting with the audience with a rhetorical stance, style, and tone that diverge from the standard academic model. Moreover, it lies in articulating something of their local circumstances as I paint larger patterns on the national canvas. That requires asking about, listening to, and being a student of people's lived experiences, being a participant in people's lives. For me, being a public scholar means being some combination of field researcher, national expert, and activist.

Increasingly, being a public scholar, for me, meant getting private inquiries about contract provisions. This was another step on the path of engagement, serving as an (unpaid) expert consultant commenting specifically on negotiation strategies and language. Barbara Bowen, president of the Professional Staff Congress (the faculty/professional staff union at the City University of New York [CUNY]), contacted me years ago about a particular contract provision being negotiated. Out of our exchanges about patterns in CBAs nationally came an idea that was successfully negotiated and subsequently enhanced the working conditions of many thousands of assistant professors in that unit.

Being an expert consultant presented no ethical challenge. My advice was based on my independent scholarly analysis of national patterns of contract language. But it constituted a different level of engagement. It made me more directly a participant, even a minor player, in negotiated terms and conditions of employment. And that spoke to my purpose, the possibility of developing counternarratives to neoliberal practices, not simply in text, but also in practice.

In 2008, an opportunity arose to serve as the general secretary for the American Association of University Professors (AAUP). With that position came a new context for thinking through choices surrounding public scholarship. I would be advocating for policies and practices about academic freedom, shared governance, and tenure and due process. I would be participating in organizing campaigns and supporting existing bargaining units. I would be a full player in organized academic labor.

Much of my credibility with the association's leadership and membership had to do with my scholarship. That was also true of my credibility with the various institutional associations (and managers) with which I would increasingly come into contact—such as monthly meetings of the Higher Education Secretariat, convened by the American Council on Education, composed of representatives of institutional and other associations (e.g., governing boards and business officers).

The public visibility of my position at AAUP meant much more consistent and deeper engagement with the media, from trade and print press to Fox News, National Public Radio, and the world of press releases. Here again, I foregrounded my scholarly expertise.

Although I was on leave from the University of Arizona, I did not take leave from my scholarship. My scholarship was simply sublimated by a mountain of managerial and advocacy work. I continued to gather data. I wrote a National Science Foundation grant that was funded. But I was now all-in as a player in policy, practice, and advocacy.

The purposes that animated my scholarly work remained. They were at the heart of why I accepted the position at AAUP. The benefits to my academic work that had accrued from my public scholarship were expanded. There was a dramatic increase in the number of campus visits, opportunities to talk with and learn from practitioners, and involvement in faculty union campaigns and contract negotiations. More than ever, the practitioners I was learning from included presidents and board members. It was as if I were conducting a two-and-a-half-year-long field ethnography of the restructuring and negotiation of academic labor amid academic capitalism.

My engagement in the world of practice was further enhanced through my participation in and presentations at the annual conferences of the National

Center for the Study of Collective Bargaining in Higher Education and the Professions (NCSCBHEP). Again, this involved a shift in rhetorical tone for a conference of practitioners that includes labor and management and presents panels on them working through issues together. This involvement fit with my larger purpose of exploring creative possibilities for negotiating the terms and conditions of work in ways that advance the public interest. It also was yet another public scholarship venue in which the quality and integrity of my academic scholarship put me in good standing.

Although my time at AAUP was rewarding, I was not able to do the research I wanted. My university leave running out, and I was in danger of losing my scholarly edge. There was a professional aspect to this situation, but also a political one, because my scholarship is at the heart of my contribution to the larger project animating my work.

As I transitioned back to a faculty position, I also transitioned into a more direct, activist role with contingent faculty, about whom I had conducted much scholarship and with whom I had increasingly worked as an ally. I became a board member of the New Faculty Majority (NFM) Foundation, an advocacy group for contingent faculty, and I spoke at the launches of several "metro campaigns" of the Service Employees International Union (SEIU) in cities around the country.

Partly, this transition was a return to my role as a scholar–expert studying contract language nationally and serving as a resource and private (unpaid) advisor for organizing and organized units of (adjunct) faculty. But it was and is more than that. I am, as an ally, part of the contingent faculty labor movement.

That dual identity of scholar–expert and ally is at the core of my increased media presence in outlets like CNN and the *New York Times*. It is expressed in academic research and publications, as well as in private communications that advance proposals for policy and practice (Rhoades 2013). With that dual identity, once again, has come a re-calibrating of rhetorical tone that is attuned to different audiences, none of which are receptive to professorial sentences with extensive modifying phrasing.

As with all of my public scholarship, this latest stage of involvement has enabled me to take my academic work into richer territory in very rewarding ways, just as the expanded database I gained access to nearly a quarter century ago did. Each stage in my engagement in public scholarship has meant choices about audience, roles and responsibilities, and the purpose of my performance, answers to the questions of to whom, how, and why I profess. In answering those questions, I make professional, ethical, and political choices. Professionally, the choices are consequential in the balance between considerations of career (as in, if I do this will it hurt or help my career) and scholarly creativity and interest. Ethically, the choices are about freedom to do one's research without censure or retaliation for designing, collecting, analyzing, and presenting scholarship, and to do instruction, service, and outreach. Politically, the choices are about the purposes and interests to which we connect our work.

Such choices are made by all scholars, not just those engaged in public scholarship, even if others are not aware of them. When a scholar gears an academic article's recommendations to particular audiences, frames research from policymakers' perspectives, informs formal decision makers, and defines problems in a way that reflects neoliberal logic, they are making choices about audience, roles and responsibilities, and purpose. When they do research on "what works," the most common form of policy work in our field, they are framing their questions based on certain assumptions regarding what works for whom and to what purposes. So, too, not doing work that is relevant to or focused on policy or practice is also a choice, with consequences in terms of being passively aligned with existing structures in academe and society.

Those of us engaged in public scholarship negotiate conventional conceptions of professional neutrality in different ways, in different contexts, at different points in time. There is value in articulating and grappling with our choices by way of self-disclosure as well as public disclosure. That is what I mean by negotiating public scholarship—an inner dialogue in which all academics should engage, for it is at the heart of our social contract with society, our role and responsibility as academics, and to whom and to what purposes we direct our work.

At this point in time, more than ever, it is incumbent on us to engage in public scholarship. As an academy, there are too many worlds that we are too little a part of. If we want respect and freedom for our higher education system and our world view of (social) science and empirical work, or if we want to influence and inform broad and particular policy arenas, then we need to be more consistently engaged in varied public arenas and communities. We need not compromise our independence to better engage non-academic audiences. But this engagement will require us to rethink our conventional stance of professional neutrality and to refine our understanding of independence as scholar–experts in order to recognize and work through our interdependence with the people and phenomena we study and should better serve.

REFERENCES

Keller, Evelyn Fox. 1985. *Reflections on gender and science.* New Haven, CT: Yale University Press.

Rhoades, Gary. 2013. "Disruptive innovations for adjunct faculty: Common sense for the common good." *Thought & Action* 29: 71–86.

Rhoades, Gary, Judy Marquez Kiyama, Rudy McCormick, and Marisol Quiroz. 2008. "Local cosmopolitans and cosmopolitan locals: New models of professionals in the academy." *Review of Higher Education* 32: 209–35.

chapter 9

Bridging the Artificial Gap between Activism and Scholarship to Form Tools for Knowledge

ESTELA MARA BENSIMON

Until 1999 I was a scholar in the traditional sense, complying with the research expectations that enabled me to move from assistant to full professor. But four years after becoming a full professor, I suddenly found myself in a professional and personal crisis, which motivated me to found the Center for Urban Education (CUE) with an explicit focus on achieving racial equity in higher education outcomes.

To best explain this crisis and how it led to the creation of CUE, I need to back up.

I came of age in the 1960s and devoted time in the early part of my career to advocating for the educational rights of the growing Puerto Rican community in New Jersey. I worked to persuade state education officials and policymakers that bilingual education was a legitimate pedagogical approach that should be available to Spanish-speaking students.

My job as the young director of education at the Puerto Rican Congress of New Jersey, a grassroots community organization, was to use information to make racial discrimination and inequity transparent and undeniable. I was not even twenty-five years old, and I am sure that I had no idea what words like "research" or "data" meant. Yet, thinking back on it, I *was* doing research—just a different kind. I pored over arcane reports produced by the New Jersey Department of Higher Education; I wrote testimony demanding greater transparency on who goes to college and where they go, disaggregated by race and ethnicity (a practice even rarer then than it is today); and I made demands for reports breaking down the racial and ethnic composition of the faculty.

In short, I learned to use data to persuade leaders into action.

It's a skill I still use today. Much of my work now revolves around data as a catalyst for practitioners to reflect on how their practices enable (or not) racial equity in educational outcomes.

At the close of the 1970s, I decided to earn my doctorate and was seduced by the luxury of a life of the mind. I say "luxury" because reading and thinking in the courtyard of Teachers College at Columbia University felt idyllic after having spent years constantly confronting the resistance of powerful policymakers and educational leaders to buy into the social justice agenda.

When I eventually joined the professoriate in the late 1980s, I took every opportunity to go out into the field to interview higher education leaders and write about the sensemaking frames of college presidents, the difference between "real" and "illusory" leadership teams, and the correspondence between presidents' espoused theories and their theories-in-use (Argyris and Schön 1974). But even then, I began to feel the pull back into an advocacy state of mind. I began to question why the theories of leadership I was drawing upon seemed all to be based on a male conception of leadership. I reanalyzed my studies of presidents' sensemaking frames from a feminist perspective and began to advocate for broadening theories of organizational change and leadership to be more inclusive of the experiences of women and people of color. Increasingly, my writings confronted traditional theories of academic leadership, socialization, and organizational change by posing the "woman" and "race" questions (Harding 1986; Nkomo 1992).

Assuming this more critical stance in my scholarship felt truer to my prior identity in community organizing. Yet, simply collecting and analyzing data was no longer satisfying to me. Studying leaders, faculty, and change initiatives was not enough. Even publishing my findings in peer-reviewed journals felt unfulfilling.

The result was a professional and personal crisis. In 1999, my work veered off in a direction that was methodologically new yet very much influenced by the values and politics that were at the center of my activist work in the 1970s. From then until today, my research agenda—embodied in the collective work of the Center for Urban Education—has been explicitly anti-racist. CUE's agenda throughout that time has remained explicitly political and race-conscious. This has changed how I am perceived by education scholars, leading to my being described as a "public scholar," though I have never described myself with that term. Some have gone so far as to accuse me of being an "activist scholar"—a label that I am happy to embrace because I don't see it as derogatory, although many do. More importantly, and relevant to the topic of this book, what distinguishes me from the traditional scholar identity is the explicitness of having an anti-racist research agenda coupled with the adaptation of research methods into tools to bring about equity-minded transformation among practitioners whose everyday practices produce and maintain racial inequity.

The anti-racist and equity-focused agenda that I set for CUE seventeen years ago shares the ideals and commitment that motivated my community-oriented advocacy with and on behalf of the Puerto Rican community in New Jersey many decades ago. Much like the community advocacy work I did in the 1970s, the work I do now as CUE's director is focused on educational equity. Both share a clear intent to dismantle institutional barriers that stand in the way of racial equity in educational access and outcomes. The methods I use now are quite different from the methods I used then, yet they are still often misunderstood.

Action research is often maligned as "not research" or as "activist research." I believe that these labels derive in part from a lack of clarity about the role the researcher plays in carrying out action research. To illustrate both the role of the action researcher and how the methods of research are deployed in action research, I can share two challenges that inspired us to create new tools: (1) how to present data showing evidence of racial inequity, which often elicits reactions of justification, and (2) how to react to expressions of direct and indirect racism among higher education practitioners that collaborate with the Center for Urban Education.

Consider the first challenge—evidence of racial inequity eliciting justification as a reaction. One tenet of praxis-oriented change is that the fundamental driving force of institutional change is when institutional actors take notice of contradictions between espoused values and actual conditions (Seo and Creed 2002). To apply this tenet to our equity-focused work at CUE, we use numerical data disaggregated by race and ethnicity to expose the pervasiveness of racial inequity in basic indicators of educational access, opportunity, and success. Our hope and expectation was that practitioners, in seeing a picture of inequality locally (i.e., within their own institutions rather than in an abstract report), would express dissatisfaction and want to take action. Racial inequity, we reasoned, represents a contradiction to values held dear in the academy, such as equality, fairness, and the democratizing purposes of education. Contrary to our expectations, however, the data showing big gaps in educational outcomes between Black and Latino students and their White counterparts often elicited explanations, justifications, and rationalizations that attempted to portray the gaps as unfortunate but not surprising—as if the gaps were natural.

The lesson for us was that, in order for inequity to be viewed as a *contradiction* to professional and institutional values, we, as action researchers, needed to create more powerful tools. This led us to create a variety of protocols to help practitioners see that racism, regardless of intent, is present in their own practices, including what they include in a syllabus, how they interact with minoritized students within and outside the classroom, what hiring and evaluation criteria they use (and how these are implicated in the failure to hire more faculty of color), and how they conduct such normative processes as program review and curriculum development (which often omit race as a criterion of quality).

To support this deeper race-conscious practitioner inquiry, we perceived a need to do more than simply present data or share protocols. We had to design tools that enable practitioners to analyze artifacts of teaching, administration, budgeting, and planning through a critical equity lens. The design of these tools has involved considerable research in theories of learning, observation methods, and discourse analysis, and has required the creative capacity to adapt theoretical concepts and research methods into inquiry tools that we can teach to practitioners quickly and that they can implement within the constraints of their schedules. While these tools serve what some may consider an activist agenda, their construction and implementation adhere rigorously to the principles and methods associated with social science research. In contrast to traditional social science research, however, our methods at the local campus level have the purpose of creating change in practices and mindsets, rather than simply reporting or measuring what is observed.

In addition to the design of theory-based tools, CUE also relies on the traditional methods of social science research, such as observations, interviews, surveys, and the examination of reconstructed artifacts, to assess the effectiveness of the tools. This assessment phase is important because, in action research, "validity, credibility, and reliability" are measured by the willingness of the participants "to act on the results of the action research" (Greenwood and Levin 2005, 54).

Looking at the second challenge, that of not knowing how to react to expressions of direct and indirect racism as action researchers, we realized that we needed a shift in how we perceived our role. Because institutional insiders conduct the actual research, our role has shifted from research producer to consultant and facilitator of action inquiry. This role requires us to be skilled in maintaining personal relationships—qualities not typically associated with research.

Of course, the need to maintain personal and respectful relationships with our partner institutions poses its own unique challenges, particularly when we are witness to racial bias and stereotyping but realize that by calling attention to this we risk offending and silencing individuals. Yet, if we don't react, we are wasting a teachable moment. As one example, in a recent meeting with the leaders of an Equity Scorecard[1] partner, a CUE staff member pointed out that African American students were more likely than other groups to enroll in math courses. The automatic response to her observation was that "they are athletes" who enroll in math to maintain their eligibility, implying that their enrollment is not because math is a priority or because they plan to pursue STEM (science, technology, engineering, and mathematics) majors. Had these students been White, the response would likely have been different, but none of the campus leaders realized the implications of their response and their dismissive tone.

At another partner college, CUE team members commented to a group of leaders that African American students were outperforming all other groups on a particular indicator of educational outcomes. Much to our surprise, the college President replied, "It is . . . because they are athletes," who receive extra academic support and therefore perform better. Two different institutions, two different scenarios—yet the same athlete stereotype was offered as a logical justification for good academic performance. In both instances, the athlete stereotype went unnoticed by the leaders. In both instances, no one questioned the lack of supporting evidence or the fact that they were making a wild generalization (as it would be highly unlikely that all African Americans—men and women—at both institutions are athletes).

Racialized explanations such as these often emerge in unrehearsed everyday talk (Perakyla 2005). CUE team members, in their role as researcher-facilitators, are often challenged by how to turn comments like these into teachable moments without offending our partners or making them feel embarrassed and defensive. We believe practitioners commit these racial offenses because they are generally unreflective about race and racism. For the most part, they do not have the foundational knowledge necessary to understand the harmful implications of casting African American students as athletes.

Our tools address topics like stereotypes, microaggressions, and racial biases. We also recognize that to be effective change agents for racial equity we need to continuously turn to research to develop better tools that are responsive to situations such as the ones just described. Experience has taught us that equity-mindedness does not come naturally. It starts with a moral commitment, but it requires a knowledge base. It takes a lot of practice. As action researchers, we apply research skills to create instructional tools to provide a scaffold around concepts such as equity-mindedness in the historical, economic, social, and cultural antecedents of racism. Our goal is not to make anyone feel defensive or embarrassed—it is to bring about a clearer understanding of the damage racism can do in the academic setting.

Is this understanding a product of "activist scholarship," which I've often been accused of undertaking? Or is this an example of spreading knowledge on a difficult topic in a way that genuinely works?

"Our ways of knowing," observes Norma Romm (2010), "are inextricably linked with our ways of living and being" (vi). I believe—and have always believed—that we can live and be better through knowledge. I would hope that all educators believe this, even when the knowledge in question is difficult to face.

As I considered the questions posed by Laura Perna for this volume, ("Why do you do the work that you do? What goals are you trying to achieve? How do your personal experiences influence your understanding of the connections between research and advocacy?"), I thought about the different stages of my living and being, from advocate to conformity to anti-racist scholarship, and the areas of knowledge that came at each of those periods of my life. Looking back, I'm grateful for the path that led to their coalescing into a practice of research that enlists social science research methods to advance an anti-racist agenda. People may call that what they wish. To me, it really is just living and being.

NOTES

1. The Equity Scorecard is CUE's signature action inquiry tool. See http://cue.usc.edu/tools /the-equity-scorecard/.

REFERENCES

Argyris, Chris, and Donald A. Schön. 1974. *Theory in practice: Increasing professional effectiveness.* San Francisco: Jossey-Bass.
Greenwood, Davydd J., and Morten Levin. 2005. "Reform of the social sciences and of univer-

sities through action research." In *The Sage handbook of qualitative research*, edited by Norman K. Denzin and Yvonna S. Lincoln, 3rd ed., 43–64. Thousand Oaks, CA: Sage.

Harding, Sandra. 1986. *The science question in feminism*. Ithaca, NY: Cornell University Press.

Nkomo, Stella M. 1992. "The emperor has no clothes: Rewriting 'Race in organizations.'" *Academy of Management Review* 17 (3): 487–513.

Perakyla, Anssi. 2005. "Analyzing talk and text." In *The Sage handbook of qualitative research*, edited by Norman K. Denzin and Yvonna S. Lincoln, 3rd ed., 869–86. Thousand Oaks, CA: Sage.

Romm, Norma. 2010. *New racism: Revisiting researcher accountabilities*. New York: Springer Science and Business Media.

Seo, Myeong-Gu, and W. E. Douglas Creed. 2002. "Institutional contradictions, praxis, and institutional change: A dialectical perspective." *Academy of Management Review* 27 (2): 222–47.

chapter 10

So That the People May Live

Research and Advocacy—from Indigenous Circles to the Public Domain

CHERYL CRAZY BULL

Being an indigenous researcher is an experience rooted in a centuries-long history of American Indian education and our experiences with the settling of North America by Europeans. It is an experience that educators and scholars must examine from an historical perspective, because to do otherwise fails to call on the influence of the victories and challenges of my ancestors. I acknowledge this historical perspective as I discuss what it means to be an indigenous researcher and advocate.

I rarely describe my career as a job. To me, my career is a calling that arose out of the dreams of my ancestors for educated Native people who work for better lives for everyone in our societies. I didn't understand this early in my path as an educator, but now I do—our tribal people have voices and knowledge, and the role of educators and researchers is to make sure those voices are heard and that knowledge is shared. There is a saying among the Lakota that we do the work we do so that the people may live. To me that is why research and advocacy are so important: so that my people may live.

Like many, I am shaped by the environment in which I grew up. I lived in the safety of an extended family that included both blood relatives and others in our community. Our community was more than our town—it was the whole Indian reservation. We had relatives and friendships everywhere. We called each other by relative names and attended ceremonies marking such occasions as birthdays, accomplishments, and name-giving. We surrounded each other during times of grief with food and generosity. The world of the Creator was always present in our traditional practices and our Christian faith.

Now that I look back, people were struggling. There were not enough jobs, housing, or adequate health care. Alcohol affected every family. Food provided through government commodities was not healthy; it had too much sugar and fat. Teachers in the schools were mostly white, and despite their care for the children in their classrooms, they didn't know anything about tribal ways and relationships, and therefore were unable to make the formal education of children meaningful.

In high school, our only forays into the indigenous world were reading American Indian literature like Scott Momaday's *The Way to Rainy Mountain*. We would do that in a special class set aside to study "Indian" Topics. No one talked about our history as Native people, and the only times we heard anything formal about ourselves in school was when we had guest speakers from the tribal government.

In the 1970s, when I was in college, faculty and other students made comments about the reservations, implying they were dangerous or making jokes about the cultural practices of tribal citizens. There were few classes about Indians, although Native studies (particularly history and Indian education) were becoming more prevalent. Students sought their place as Natives through clubs and social events. The renaissance of tribal cultures and traditions was underway but had not reached the halls of state higher education institutions. No one studied Indians. We were preserved through artifacts and taped interviews. This disconnect from who we were was pervasive, and it influenced my later commitment to my work as an educator and researcher.

I completed college in 1981 and went back to my reservation to live. A gift arrived in the form of a job at our tribal college. From there, in the heart of cultural practice, storytelling, and relationships, came my own understanding of indigenous scholarship and research. I realized that the transition of tribal peoples into modern society did not have to be a transition to assimilation. Indeed, our people had resisted hundreds of years of federal policy intended to remove our cultural and ethnic identity. We were not going to become like others in America—lost to our teachings about who we are or barren of our languages and ways of knowing. But we were struggling with the transitions required of us to be prosperous and healthy. I discovered that the movement for tribally controlled education had the answers to the challenges that adapting to modern life presented. Tribally controlled education through indigenous scholarship and research is about the restoration of who we are. It is key to our self-determination as individuals and as a people.

As indigenous people we adapted research to respond to the transitions I just described. As researchers we had to create a research process that is both familiar and meaningful through strategies that connect our voice with the complexities of information and its interpretation. We do this when we participate in modern research practices, such as a study of medical interventions that includes traditional medicines. In that context, my goal as an educator and researcher is to help with the translation of our traditional ways into contemporary environments. The path of this translation requires courage. What I consider an opportunity that reinforces identity and self-determination may be viewed as a threat by those accustomed to established approaches to research. So there is risk of confrontation or disregard when Native researchers and allies promote the use of integrated indigenous knowledge or the use of indigenous knowledge as the foundation to approaching the acquisition or sharing of knowledge.

In an academic environment that didn't appreciate or foster indigenous research, courageous acts took place to bring attention to our research and scholarship. For example, in 1989 I attended a meeting of Native researchers hosted by the *Tribal College Journal* (*TCJ*). In an essay discussing the meeting published by *TCJ*, I shared the remarkable recognition of indigenous scholarship that the meeting afforded. Prior to that meeting, my role as an educator focused on finding the knowledge and the ways that we could teach in order to preserve our way of life. Before we became broadly knowledgeable about indigenous research and evaluation methodologies, we focused on gathering information from oral and written sources and on finding ways to teach classes that shared this knowledge through our tribal colleges. We were just beginning to understand that our knowledge is fundamental and can be the foundation of all curriculum and instructional practice. We were just coming into our own understanding of an indigenous pedagogy. However, our own, defined pedagogy is not possible without research and scholarship.

While tribal college scholars were gathering knowledge and developing approaches to teaching in our communities, indigenous scholars across the country were gathering to influence the changing landscape of indigenous research in higher education. Their work greatly influenced my own practices and my commitment to research. These scholars organized themselves to promote the inclusion of indigenous researchers in conferences and publications, and in teaching and research positions in the academy. Noted indigenous scholars Karen Swisher, John Tippeconnic, Dave Beaulieu, Elizabeth Cook Lynn, Linda Tuwahi Smith, Carmelita Lamb, and Daniel Wildcat, as well as our late scholars Vine Deloria Jr. and John Mohawk, are among those who inform our thinking about indigenous research and scholarship through their examinations of the role of research in tribal society. These intellectual leaders remind us of the obligation that we have as indigenous researchers to engage in study that is relevant to our indigenous identities and to our survival. They offer not only thoughtful encouragement, but also approaches that can be used to "stay in the place" of our identity and our survival. The practices of community-based participatory research resonate with their advice and expectations. These scholars also reinforce our belief that knowledge comes not only from observation and instruction, but also from our spiritual practices.

There are many paths for research. To me, Native higher education research should be rooted in fostering the ability of our people succeed in both their educational experiences and their efforts to help transform our communities. Our scholars are not just responsible for being good stewards of their role in the academy; they are also responsible for helping our people live.

We live lives of extreme dichotomies, and indigenous researchers have a duty to advocate for personal and tribal self-determination to ameliorate those dichotomies. The indigenous population in the United States—American Indians, Alaska Natives, and Native Hawaiians—is a small population whose characteristics are unique in both geographic and cultural contexts and whose socio-demographics are painfully disheartening. Indigenous people have the highest infant mortality rate and the lowest life expectancy, and they are the least likely to complete high school and college. These conditions exist within rich and abundant ways of living that offer incredible resources for success. We have thousands of years of tribal knowledge to lead us to better lives.

Research is a tool to generate knowledge that addresses the disparities that exist among our people and to strengthen our families and communities. Research informs ways to improve education through better curriculum and well-trained teachers, to improve health through prevention and intervention in matters that are influenced by lifestyles and economic issues, and to produce better systems of care. We have to step out of existing research paradigms where research is used to study lives rather than improve lives in order to address the dichotomies in our societies.

Advocacy in this environment is a critical necessity. Advocacy is using our knowledge through our voices as speakers, writers, and collaborators to tell the stories of ourselves so we are not the "other" but are rather "ourselves" as citizens. As indigenous educators, we call attention to how our ways of knowing influence our quality of life. Because of the tremendous influence that our history has on our understanding of our world and because of the remarkable changes that have occurred due to technology, tribal scholarship and research can provide us with the knowledge and tools we need to accomplish that advocacy. We know what we need to lead better lives—research helps us define that and then contributes to transformative change through practice, policy, and advocacy.

Equally necessary is ensuring that research and advocacy are a public experience. When I think of the role of higher education researchers in the context of the public intellectual, I am reminded of the visionary goal of higher education desired by the founders of the tribal college movement. Their goal was nothing less than the transformation of troubled families and communities into culturally grounded, socially dynamic, and economically thriving healthy ones. I have no doubt that this requires advocacy from a place of deep understanding and with an intention of correcting moral wrongs. It is wrong to create and maintain educational systems that diminish identity and confidence rather than building them up. It is wrong for tribal higher education to be woefully underfunded and for tribal colleges to not have decent facilities and adequate equipment. Public intellectuals in both the indigenous community and in other higher education communities must be willing to speak up, armed with knowledge, to advocate for the vital improvements and resources needed for tribal higher education to fulfill the vision of the movement's founders and to address social injustices.

Throughout the many organizations that work in research and related fields, such as evaluation and communities of practices, a strong, emergent, and creative cadre of practitioners is adapting our traditional approaches to contemporary experiences and, most importantly, advocating that our ways of knowing—oral traditions, stories, experiences, and observations—are valid and reliable research and advocacy tools. These practitioners are the public intellectuals who are examining and producing information in higher education, research, and theory.

Because I have spent most of my thirty-five-year career in tribal higher education, I am particularly focused on how we as higher education advocates can use the knowledge of our people to create greater opportunities and generate more resources for our families and societies. There are characteristics and qualities of the lives of indigenous people that require our attention to accomplish our goal of improved quality of life among tribal citizens. These characteristics and qualities include the following:

1. An understanding that each of our tribes has its own creation story and its own teachings about how to live on the earth and how to be a good relative.

2. Recognition that our skills include being able to interpret through observation and experience how to appropriately use the resources available to us, especially in a manner that is sensitive to critical issues such as climate change.

3. Acceptance of the life cycle and its teachings for each tribe. We are skilled in our ability to bring young children into the human world, and through our teachings we are able to help them in all passages of life and to be supportive of all of our identities.

4. Belief that education is both a tool of assimilation and an opportunity to ground our identities. Thus, tribally controlled education is essential to achieving our vision of prosperity.

We believe the path to social justice and prosperity requires that all indigenous people are able to have their unique tribal identities, to take care of themselves and their families, to have high-quality governance, and to have access to the resources that will ensure our survival for the next 10,000 years.

In a civil society, which I believe is the heritage of indigenous people, all who have something to contribute to decision making are heard through dialogue that is inclusive within the context of each tribal group. Sometimes the role of these contributors is to share knowledge that can be used to make decisions; sometimes their role is to be an advocate for making a decision in a certain way. In both situations, the holders of our knowledge must speak from a place of understanding that comes from research and experience. Today, higher education researchers and advocates find themselves in these roles. Sometimes their role is to share information that helps those in policy-making and resource allocation positions to make decisions. Sometimes their role is to share information that influences those decisions in ways that achieve the broader goals of society and higher education.

The success of tribal colleges and universities and the return on investment experienced by individuals and tribes are evidence that education is the answer to the many challenges faced by tribes today. Higher education access has increased the employment of graduates in environments of high unemployment. We are better stewards of our environment and natural resources. Curriculum development and teacher training have dramatically changed schooling for our children. Research has made it possible for us to do our work and to know the value of the investment in our work.

We often use the imagery of a circle to describe our understanding of the world. The circle represents our continuous relationship with each other and with Creation. We strive to have that circle be unbroken. When I think of our work as indigenous public intellectuals and advocates, I think of a circle where our people stand in the middle and we surround them with all of the knowledge and resources that they need to lead good lives. We make this circle so that the people may live.

chapter 11

My People's Professor

Research for the Humanization and Liberation of Black Americans

SHAUN R. HARPER

My people need advocates. They need smart, well-positioned Black intellectuals to use what we know to advance liberation and dismantle oppressive systems that have disadvantaged our families across generations. Less valuable to them are dispassionate academic projects that fall short of presenting full truths about the myriad ways in which institutionalized manifestations of racism negatively affect our lives, schools, and communities. Pointless studies that reach no further than the pages of peer-reviewed academic journals, decontextualized studies produced by those who know too little about us, and studies that mistreat us as variables instead of people are not what my people need or want. They need and want justice, fairness, equity, and respect. They expect extraordinarily gifted Black academics with doctorates to leverage our research to engender systemic change in a nation that has cyclically failed our families, from slavery through Jim Crow and into the twenty-first century. They are proud of our academic accomplishments and educational attainment, but with that pride comes reasonably high expectations for service to our families and communities. Understandably, they do not really care whether we get tenure or earn the respect of our White faculty colleagues. The needs for justice in our communities are too urgent to do our academic work in culturally unresponsive and socially irresponsible ways. Recognizing that I am my people's professor is the reason I do my work in the ways I do it.

My People vs. the Academy

I somehow understood early in my faculty career that adhering to certain cultural norms of the academy would best position me to amass the power and gain access to the platforms necessary to become the most influential version of my people's professor. I have strategically identified ways to resolve tensions between the expectations of the academy and my people's expectations of me. For instance, I publish my work in peer-reviewed journals, which I actually enjoy because of the helpful feedback I receive from anonymous colleagues and journal editors. Nothing in my field is more valued than publishing in peer-reviewed journals. Hence, I will continue doing so for the rest of my career. Notwithstanding this commitment, I know that publishing my work in venues the White architects and gatekeepers of my field most cherish, on its own, does far too little to liberate my people. Throughout my career, even as an untenured assistant professor, I have sought to address this in four ways.

First, I make peace with publishing in peer-reviewed journals to which my people have limited access by doing the best I can to execute rigorous research methods, generate and advance theory, and produce sensible, forward-thinking implications for policy and practice. These things satisfy the nerd in me who spends dozens of hours meticulously crafting each article. But they are also important because having other scholars cite and effectively build on my work ultimately helps my people. My studies have been cited in more than 7,500 academic publications, which bolsters my credibility and advances what the field knows about minoritized[1] peoples, equity, justice, success, and liberation. Citations are important to me for one additional reason: they position a Black scholar among the intellectual heavyweights in my field. It is essential that graduate students and early career scholars see researchers like themselves on the rosters of the most highly cited papers. I care more about this for them than I do for my own self-aggrandizement.

Second, I strategically disseminate my peer-reviewed journal articles. Eight years ago, I created a website on which all my articles are available in PDF format at no charge.[2] To date, these publications have been downloaded over 100,000 times from that website. As soon as new articles are released, I tweet and post announcements to Facebook, as well as send e-mail messages to the nearly 10,000 website subscribers. Some may misinterpret this as self-promotion, but it has been my way of promoting the research to ensure as many people as possible have access to it. My people are especially proud when they see on social media that I have published a new study about them. Titles of my papers often confirm for them that I am upholding my commitment to Black liberation.

Translating my peer-reviewed studies for a range of audiences is a third way in which I counterbalance publishing in journals the academy values. In my view, studies are worthless if people cannot understand them or do not have access to them. I present my research at annual meetings of the Association for the Study of Higher Education and the American Educational Research Association (which the academy values), as well as at the annual conferences of the National Association of Student Personnel Administrators and other national meetings that thousands of practitioners who work with college students attend. Beyond this, I base just about every keynote I deliver on a campus or elsewhere on my research. Moreover, I have presented the same research that I have published in journals to hundreds of Black and Latino families in Philadelphia, Camden, New York, Los Angeles, and other cities. Those families see me as an advocate, their advocate, our advocate. In this way, I concurrently do what my people and the academy value.

Lastly, universities value positive press. My research has been featured and I have been quoted in the *New York Times*, *Washington Post*, *Wall Street Journal*, *Sports Illustrated*, *Chronicle of Higher Education*, *Inside Higher Ed*, and over 11,000 news outlets across the United States and abroad. I have been interviewed on CNN, ESPN, NPR, and dozens of other television and radio networks. I hear from my people immediately after I appear on television—they call, send emails, and use social media to express their pride and gratitude. That I am an advocate is obvious to anyone who reads my quoted statements in news stories or listens to what I say in interviews. To the greatest extent possible, I ground my advocacy in my own and others' research. I resist making statements to journalists that I cannot preface with "my research shows" or, at the very least, "some studies show." I have also attempted to shape public opinion through the publication of a handful of op-eds. Even in these, my opinions are substantiated by research I have conducted. My university profits tremendously from the positive attention my advocacy produces in the press. Were I a disimpassioned scholar who had no compelling insights to offer from my research, I am certain that fewer journalists would include my perspectives and my university's name in their news stories. Most important to me is using mainstream media platforms to represent the needs and voices of my people and to humanize them for those who view us as uneducable and less than human.

Humanizing Endarkened Variables

In communicating my research to a range of audiences, I aim to disrupt racist, one-sided, deficit-oriented, criminalized, and hopeless misrepresentations of my people. I maintain here, as I have done elsewhere, that George Zimmerman murdered Trayvon Martin because he had been socialized to believe that a Black male teen in a predominantly White neighborhood did not belong there and was likely a criminal. As a Black intellectual, I know I can do *something* about the murder of unarmed Black folks (both the actual loss of life and the death of their educational aspirations in racist schooling situations). Beyond using my platform to protest the miscarriage of justice and educational malpractice, I have assumed responsibility for helping our nation and world see the good in my people, to recognize that almost all Black Americans desire to succeed and thrive despite the odds stacked against us since slavery.

I am Black and male. So too are my father, husband, siblings, nephews, and most of my closest friends, fraternity brothers, mentors, and mentees. I owe it to them and to all other Black boys and men to be an advocate—a serious, credible, and reliable one—who tells their full truths. It would be personally fraudulent and professionally reckless to read only bad news about Black men and not use my research to offer a more complete picture of us. Failure to do so, particularly in rigorously qualitative ways, would make me complicit in the perpetuation of the research missteps that I often critique. Researchers frequently mistreat Black Americans and other minoritized populations as variables in their statistical models. They then go on to make all sorts of assumptions about my people vis-à-vis Whites and other groups in their analyses. Much about this is dehumanizing. Scholars who have never been inside our homes or walked streets in our neighborhoods, who have spent little time inside our schools, and who have few substantive interactions with Blacks outside of workplace settings often reinforce hopelessly dark narratives about us. Many who build their careers on studying us often do not really know us. To them we are variables, not people with complex lives worthy of deep, authentic understanding and humanistic representation.

I am frustrated by how so-called experts (sometimes other scholars of color) use statistics to talk about my people in such dark ways. Statistics have some value, as they offer particular ways of knowing. I am appreciate quantitative analyses and sometimes use statistics in my research. At the same time, I repeatedly endure an agonizing experience in Washington, DC. I am occasionally invited to speak on panels at the White House and talk to policymakers on Capitol Hill, which is a real honor and privilege. The topics are usually focused on access and equity in education, sometimes specifically on boys and men of color. I am almost always the only non-White person on these panels and the only panelist sharing findings from qualitative studies. Well-intended White scholars talk mostly about what their and other researchers' quantitative analyses show. In so doing, they reinforce, perhaps unintentionally, certain notions about my people: our schools and communities are terrible, our families do not value education, and our futures are bleak. They present statistical trends. I present my people's voices and recognize our humanity. I find surprising how powerfully my approach resonates with DC audiences (congresspersons, education policy advisors, directors of White House initiatives, etc.). Because they keep inviting me back and seeking my counsel, I believe these policy actors see me as both a credible researcher and trusted ambassador for communities of color. Advocacy is clearly evidenced in the research-based advice I offer and in the language I use to communicate findings from studies of my people.

Plainspoken Truths

As my people's professor, I write and speak plainly about them. I convey, as honestly as I know how, the insights they share with me in interviews and focus groups. At just about every college and university at which I conduct racial climate studies, minoritized students, faculty, and staff cry as they recall and describe the deeply painful encounters they have with racism on campus. I advocate for them by representing their pain (and, in some instances, trauma) in the reports I write to their institutional leaders and in the publications that my center colleagues and I produce from their data. In a *Review of Higher Education* article, I critique what I called "semantic alternatives to the words *racism* and *racist*" (Harper 2012, 20)—terms like "chilly climate." Participants in our studies do not characterize their campus climates as chilly; many say the environments and several people in them are racist. In reports and publications, I say what they said, in the words they said it.

Advocacy is perhaps most plainly spoken in the title of my article "Niggers No More." I use one of the most racially derogatory words in America to explain the following:

> Being called a Nigger, especially by a White person, usually incites emotional hurt and a range of other injurious feelings within the insulted Black person. It is possible that being continually treated like a Nigger engenders a stronger, more cumulatively aggravating series of responses than simply being called one. Protecting readers from the penetration of this word and all that is asso-

ciated with it (historically and presently) seemed unfair to those of us who are persistently harmed by it in schools, colleges, and society. (Harper 2009, 699)

I also wrote in a *Review of Research in Education* article about Black students being "niggered" on predominantly white campuses (Harper 2013). I do not throw this term around to be provocative. Honestly, it most plainly captures what many Black people tell me they feel and experience. While I have not used the N-word on White House panels or in meetings with college presidents and their cabinet members, I consistently name needs and experiences as my people voice them in our studies. I also truthfully represent my people in keynote addresses and presentations about their racial realities. No compliment means more to me than someone who says at the end of one of my speeches, "You just spoke truth to my experience." They often do so with tears in their eyes and with the sincerest expressions of gratitude. This compels me to continue using my platform to advocate for people who have voices that others refuse to hear or take seriously.

I do not think of advocacy and academic rigor as being mutually exclusive. It is unlikely that my people had anything to do with the initial manufacturing of this false dichotomy in higher education scholarship. Research and rigor, at least in my life and career, are culturally linked. Weak, suspect studies and outrageous claims grounded in nothingness are a disservice to my people. I will never undermine my people's high expectations of me by publishing pointless, dispassionate studies about them; by conducting research that families and community members, policymakers, practitioners, and other researchers deem useless and insufficiently rigorous; or by speaking about their lives and experiences in sanitized, untruthful ways. While I am staunchly committed to advancing my field and generating new knowledge, I am most devoted to using my research and privileged position to advocate for justice on behalf of my people. I am proudly theirs. Our liberation is my highest personal and professional priority.

NOTES

1. I use "minoritized" instead of "minority" to signify the social construction of underrepresentation and subordination in U.S. social institutions, including colleges and universities. Persons are not born into a minority status nor are they minoritized in every social milieu (e.g., their families, racially homogeneous friendship groups, or places of religious worship). Instead, they are rendered minorities in particular situations and institutional environments that sustain an overrepresentation of whiteness.

2. I secure copyright clearances before posting publications to my Bepress website (https://works.bepress.com/sharper).

REFERENCES

Harper, Shaun R. 2009. "Niggers no more: A critical race counternarrative on Black male student achievement at predominantly white colleges and universities." *International Journal of Qualitative Studies in Education* 22: 697–712.

Harper, Shaun R. 2012. "Race without racism: How higher education researchers minimize racist institutional norms." *Review of Higher Education* 36: 9–29.

Harper, Shaun R. 2013. "Am I my brother's teacher? Black undergraduates, peer pedagogies, and racial socialization in predominantly white postsecondary contexts." *Review of Research in Education* 37: 183–211.

chapter 12

Listening to Students

SARA GOLDRICK-RAB

When my research team and I first met Susan, she was living in her car. It was difficult to find ways to mask that fact so that she could attend class without being disruptive. She didn't have enough to eat, let alone a place to shower or wash her clothes. She was embarrassed to let fellow students or teachers know what was happening in her life. We were among the first to learn of her situation.

When we met Chloe, we were sitting in a cafeteria surrounded by students consuming vast quantities of french fries. I wondered why she looked uncomfortable. An hour later, during an interview, she revealed that she never ate lunch because she lacked the money.

When we met Tony, he was shaken up. Like Susan he was living in his car, and the night before he had been surprised when a man pointed a gun through his window, waking him and demanding that he leave. Suffice it to say, he was not focused on his psychology exam the next morning.

Susan, Chloe, and Tony are college students whom my team of academic researchers has encountered during studies over the past decade. We never intended to study food and housing insecurity in higher education. We were trying to learn about how financial aid affects college graduation rates. But these issues and the students found us. And they told us their stories.

Many higher education policies fail to accomplish their goals, and one reason is that their approaches are often misaligned with the experiences and needs of the people they aim to affect. If we want to create effective policies that help more students to complete degrees, then we must begin by getting to know the students. Unfortunately, among today's scholars, careful and close listening is fairly uncommon. Most research these days, and especially the most influential research, is quantitative. Students are reduced to numeric data points, and their "relevant" attributes are only those that are available in low-cost administrative datasets. Test scores, grades, number of classes attempted, "expected family contribution"—these are stuff that narratives about college experiences are made of. Colleges do not ask students whether they have a stable place to live or enough to eat, and so their basic needs security is not part of the story.

Until we finally ask—or they simply tell us.

What Then?

Susan, Chloe, and Tony's stories are heartbreaking, gut-wrenching, dramatic narratives that would capture anyone. They could make us reach into our pockets and provide money, offer a bed for the night, or cook a meal. All of these are appropriate, respectable things to do. But the job of scholar-activists goes far beyond those short-term actions. Instead, our goal must be to *learn*, *evaluate*, and *act*. These three activities are integral parts of a career in scholar-activism. None of them undermines the other. And all are required to effectively do *justice* to the realities of peoples' lives.

We listen to students and act on what they teach us in pursuit of understandings that go beyond any one person, but are built one student at a time. To find ways to effectively lower the price of college, my teammates at the Wisconsin HOPE Lab conducted deep qualitative research, statistical analyses, *and* policy investigations in order situate and contextualize each individual story we are told. Doing this puts the stories in relief, surrounded by other narratives and by the policies, practices, and institutions that create them. How and why does material hardship befall some students and not others? What enables some students to get help while others experience scarcity? What is it like to navigate multiple bureaucracies while pursuing an education? Posing and addressing questions like these has helped us see that food and housing insecurity in college are, as sociologist C. Wright Mills (1967) put it, not a private trouble but rather a public issue. That means that these issues can and must be addressed by changing social policies and institutions.

Is it our job as scholars to pursue those changes? I think so. It is essential to not only unearth problems but also discover how policies and practices can be reshaped to effectively alleviate barriers. This is why I have studied welfare policy, housing and food policies, and, of course, financial aid. With randomized controlled trials, mixed-methods implementation evaluations, and pre/post designs, I consider impacts, moderators, and mediators, as well as issues of fidelity of implementation.

I then develop ideas about how to create positive change. For some that means writing white papers, and my team often does that. But we have also gone further, engaging with college administrators, legislators at both the state and federal levels, social service agencies, and a variety of other stakeholders. In meeting after meeting, we urge these stakeholders to listen to students and to *do something*. We put forth policy proposals and advocate that they be pursued.

Does this make us advocates? More importantly, does it compromise our status as researchers, perhaps rendering us less objective? I believe such questions are at best irrelevant and at worst harmful. They are irrelevant because they represent an effort by academics and the public to draw a box around intellectuals, so as to contain them. They are harmful, especially when proffered by fellow academics, because they inhibit the creative process so important to scientific discovery.

The finest public intellectuals span boundaries to go where questions take them. Public intellectuals do not adhere to methodological purity, believing that one sort of quantitative or qualitative tool is always the best or without flaws. Nor do we overly subscribe to disciplinary norms, which can constrain the development of concepts that reach beyond what sociologists or economists tend to believe. The best way to learn how to solve social problems is by not only reading and researching but also doing. Those who *do*, learn.

That is why I try to do as much as possible in higher education to contribute to my identity as a scholar-activist:

- I directly engage with practical problems and efforts to improve the world.
- I put new issues on the research agenda as well as the public agenda.
- I speak truth to power and speak truth directly to the people.
- I confront and make difficult choices every single day.
- I act with accountability to the publics I study, and I reciprocate.

For example, working to find ways to create affordable housing near college campuses helped me understand fractures in the nation's public housing system and conflicts between higher education policy and housing policy. Efforts to offer free food to undergraduates helped me learn about the powerful business interests engaged in college cafeterias, provided a window into the unintended consequences of using means-tested voucher systems versus universal approaches, and taught me about nutrition. I am also learning how to do new things as a researcher. For example, I have learned participatory action research techniques so that, together with homeless undergraduates, I can seek more effective remedies.

One of the biggest challenges my team now faces is advancing a policy agenda to expand the social safety net and connect it to higher education policies in an era when both federal and state governments are led by conservative forces that seek to cut such support. Force and stamina will be required, as well as a careful focus, for we aim to do more than simply advocate. There is nothing wrong with advocacy. I work with advocates and am amazed at their power to create change. But I wish to leverage the power not of advocacy, but of scholar-activism. What is the difference? As I wrote for *Contexts*, "An advocate begins with a core and guiding goal—not a theory—and pushes for changes to achieve that goal. In contrast, a scholar-activist begins with a set of testable assumptions, subjects these to rigorous research, and once in possession of research findings seeks to translate those findings into action . . . I much prefer the latter role since I often have more unanswered questions than clear goals, prefer to turn to data rather than personal beliefs when thinking through policy options, and find that actions are more effective when guided by research" (Goldrick-Rab 2014, n.p.).

Working as a scholar-activist in the academy has yielded many lessons, some of which were quite painful. As a person of great privilege, I cannot ask you to feel sorry for me because of the volume of hate mail and calls I have endured—I only want you to know that it has happened. Vacations have been ruined, tears shed, and pounds gained, and, yes, I have questioned my place in the academy and even the world more broadly. I have learned about the insecurities that pervade higher education administrators, the overt and covert ways in which activism is suppressed, and the lengths to which colleagues will go in order to maintain their power. But by creating and teaching a graduate-level seminar on scholar-activism, I also learned about the strong desires of younger scholars to build a better academy that recognizes, praises, and lifts up activism. That has given me hope.

I have also tried to learn about the challenges that philanthropists face as I seek to find new ways to reciprocate with students. Obviously, their immediate needs do not abate while they await the results of our research studies, and I have found it difficult to carry their stories around in my mind without doing more to help them. For years, I provided money, food, and clothing directly to the students who asked for it. But the need is tremendous, and some students—understandably enmeshed in the perils of their daily lives—demand more than my personal resources can bear. When I have been unable to deliver, I have been punished in ways that leave me skittish about entering into such personal relationships. Instead, I now work with several colleagues to operate an emergency fund for students, with money delivered by teachers to students around the country. This has been a new form of scholar-activism for me, and while it feels good, it also brings new challenges. For example, setting up the FAST Fund taught me about the difficult decisions involved in effectively stewarding funds while also delivering support to students quickly. It has also caused me to face the disheartening, never-ending need that so many colleges and universities encounter every day.

Scholar-activism requires mentoring from a family of supporters who understand what is involved. I have been fortunate to have many people to guide me, including Mike Rose, Estela Bensimon, Phil Goff, and Eve Tuck. They have taught me how to protect myself within the academy, how to get up each day and continue when it feels too hard, and how to celebrate when victories arise. I listened especially well to their advice about being honest and transparent in my daily life, which is why I choose not to inhabit separate identities as "Sara the scholar" and "Sara the person." Separating my actions and my scholarship (or even my Twitter accounts) would be false and disingenuous. Why sit in an academic conference and pretend that research is not political and that the knowledge we create isn't intended to *do something*? Why waste the time?

Certainly, scholar-activism is risky. I did not wait to begin this work until I was tenured simply because this work is part of why I am a scholar in the first place. Junior scholars who feel as I do must acknowledge, however, that activism may cause them to lose the home for their scholarship. The academy remains rife with resistance to this sort of work. But when, as higher education researchers, we take students' time and we listen to them, we also create an obligation to respond. We learn from them, and they teach us things that help us know more. I know plenty as a higher education scholar that I would not know if I were not also an activist. And I say things, and believe it is also important to say these things, that I would not say if this were not my role.

My advice for the scholar-activist brewing in you is to commit to your love of this work, to honor it, and to wake up to it every morning. Being brave requires remembering why you act. Your pursuit of excellence in research will be fulfilling and also exhausting, and yet you need to match it with efforts to create change. For me, this has never felt optional. As researchers, my team and I asked students to help us learn. They taught us. They were hungry and even homeless. So in a sense, what happened next—our emergence as scholar-activists—was never a choice. It was a moral imperative. Today it is, in every way imaginable, my life's work.

REFERENCES

Goldrick-Rab, Sara. 2014. "On scholarly activism." *Contexts*, December 4. https://contexts.org /blog/on-scholarly-activism/.

Mills, C. Wright. 1967. *Power, politics and people: The collected essays of C. Wright Mills.* Edited by Irving Louis Horowitz. New York: Oxford University Press.

chapter 13

Why Racial Microaggressions Matter

How I Came to Answer That Question and Why I Do the Work I Do

DANIEL G. SOLORZANO

In a revision of this essay, the editor, Laura Perna, asked me to write about my motivation for the work I do. I trust the answer to that question should be clear by the end of this essay. Professor Troy Duster has been credited with the following quote, "If you scratch a theory, you find a biography" (quoted in Torres 1998, 12). Throughout my forty-four-year career in higher education I have worked in various forms of race and ethnic studies theory. For the past twenty-four years, I have been working in the field of critical race theory (CRT). I define CRT as the work of scholars who are developing an explanatory framework that accounts for the role of race and racism in education. CRT works toward identifying and challenging racism in its historical and contemporary forms as part of a larger goal of identifying and challenging all forms of subordination. Using a variation of Duster's axiom, I add, "If you scratch a theory, you find an autobiography," and share my autobiography as it relates to my work in CRT and racial microaggressions, as well as why I do this work.

I came to CRT through my family, community, and religious history. I was born in 1949 and influenced by the times and the people who guided me in developing my values, beliefs, and actions. For instance, in elementary school, the Dominican Sisters instilled in me the value of helping others less fortunate. In high school, the Christian Brothers continued my training with their mission to stand with the poor. At the university level, I was influenced by the Jesuit mission of "Educating men [and I would add women] in service to others" and the "preferential option for the poor."[1] Through the rituals and beliefs of the Catholic Church, I was reminded in scripture, stories, and deeds—repeated year in and year out—that you had to give of yourself to others less fortunate. This was Catholic social teaching (CST). At a time when I was developing my own racial/ethnic and political identity in college (1968–1972), the CST around service to others, standing with the poor, and the principles of social justice were consistent with the social movements of the time. I became involved with the Chicano anti-war movement, the United Farmworker movement, and activist movements around educational equity.

If you use traditional definitions of civic engagement, such as participation in mainstream politics and organizations, then I wasn't civically engaged as a young adult. However, I was taught that civic engagement was participating in movements for social justice for those less fortunate. We don't often think of civic engagement in that way, but that is how I was trained in CST and the social movements of the time. This form of civic engagement taught me civic values grounded in social justice—a willingness to engage in the struggle to dismantle structures of inequality as an activist and a scholar. This is how I came to do social justice work. These teachings and principles continue to guide my research and activism. I do this work because I want to affect the lives of people at the margins of society.

How I Came to Do Research on Racial Microaggressions

My research on racial microaggressions is a continuation of this story. As I was discovering the work of critical race theorists in the law, in 1993, I came across an article in the *Yale Law Journal* by Peggy Davis (1989) entitled "Law as Microaggression." Davis's article was the first time I saw the word "microaggression" used in either a title or a narrative. She defined microaggressions as "stunning, automatic acts of disregard that stem from unconscious attitudes of white superiority and constitute a verification of black inferiority" (1576). She cited the origins of this concept in the work of Chester Pierce.[2] Pierce and his colleagues (1978, 66) defined microaggressions as "subtle, stunning, often automatic, and non-verbal exchanges which are 'put downs' of blacks by offenders. The offensive mechanisms used against blacks often are innocuous. The cumulative weight of their never-ending burden is the major ingredient in black-white interactions." The Davis article, the Pierce citations, and this definition started me on a journey to find, understand, and utilize the concept of racial microaggressions in my research and teaching. I went on to read (and re-read) all the works of Chester Pierce. Indeed, I wanted to know how and why he came to work on microaggressions. In 1994, I re-analyzed data I had gathered on Ford Foundation Minority Fellows using the analytical tool of racial microaggressions. I used CRT as a framework to examine of how racial and gender microaggressions affect the career paths of these Chicana and Chicano scholars. In 1998, I published an article based on these Ford scholars in the *International Journal of Qualitative Studies in Education* entitled "Critical Race Theory, Racial and Gender Microaggressions, and the Experiences of Chicana and Chicano Scholars."[3] As far as I can tell, other than the works of Pierce and his colleagues, this article was the first to empirically examine racial microaggressions.[4]

In December 1999, Walter Allen asked me to be part of a research team working on the *Grutter v. Bollinger* (539 U.S. 306) affirmative action case on behalf of the student intervenors.[5] We conducted campus climate studies at the University of Michigan Law School and its four major undergraduate feeders: University of Michigan, Michigan State University, Harvard University, and University of California, Berkeley (see Allen and Solorzano 2001). As the case was making its way through the lower federal courts and onto the US Supreme Court, and as part of our commitment to the various communities that supported the student intervenors in the *Grutter* case, Allen's team traveled to Michigan to present our findings. At one of these meetings in 2001, we finished our presentation on campus climate generally and racial microaggressions in particular to a large group made up of University of Michigan students and faculty and Detroit high school students. As the audience lined up to ask questions, a young African American high school student came to the microphone. She stood there crying. When she finally spoke, she said, "You've given me a name for my pain." This comment has remained with me for many years. This young woman expressed the raw and real feelings many people of color, from many different age groups, communities, and walks of life, have since shared with me. This young woman showed us that these two words, *racial microaggressions*, are a powerful way to acknowledge the everyday pain and suffering that people of color experience—giving voice to those at the margins.

Research and Publications

Since those first articles on racial microaggressions, I have continued to work with colleagues on empirical and conceptual manuscripts. Our work on racial microaggressions has included publications on a second affirmative action federal court case in California (*Castaneda et al. v. UC Regents et al.*, United States Federal Court, Northern District of California. Case No. C 99–0525 SI) (see Solorzano, Allen, and Carroll 2002), African American and Latina/o undergraduate students (Solorzano, Ceja, and Yosso 2000; Yosso et al. 2009), racial battle fatigue (Smith, Yosso, and Solorzano 2006), teachers (Kohli and Solorzano 2012; Ledesma and Solorzano 2013), visual microaggressions (Perez Huber and Solorzano 2015a), microaggressions as research tools (Perez Huber and Solorzano 2015b), microaggressions and social work pedagogy (Perez Huber and Solorzano, in press), and encyclopedia entrees and policy briefs (Perez Huber and Solorzano 2015c; Solorzano and Perez Huber 2012).

The UCLA Moreno Report

On Friday October 18, 2013, Gene Block, the chancellor of the University of California, Los Angeles, emailed the UCLA community an external report entitled "Independent Investigative Report on Acts of Bias and Discrimination Involving Faculty at the University of California, Los Angeles" (Moreno et al. 2013). This report has become known as the Moreno Report—named after the chair of the committee, retired California Supreme Court Justice Carlos Moreno. Chancellor Block pointed out that the Moreno Report contained some sobering and disturbing accounts of bias and discrimination some faculty of color had experienced at UCLA. The report mentioned some of our work on microaggressions. It stated,

> Several faculty members referenced the notion of "*microaggressions*," which researchers have defined as "subtle verbal and nonverbal insults directed toward non-Whites, often done automatically and unconsciously. They are layered insults based on one's race, gender, class, sexuality, language, immigration status, phenotype, accent, or surname." It is not clear to us whether any workable definition of discriminatory conduct is capable of capturing every such *microaggression* experienced by a minority faculty member ... Heightened awareness of the issue of racially insensitive conduct may help to reduce *microaggressions* or other subtle behaviors that degrade the work environment for faculty of color. (Moreno et al. 2013, 20–21; emphasis mine).

The Moreno Report shook, and continues to affect, the UCLA campus. Since the report was released, I have been asked to present my work to faculty, students, and staff in numerous departments, schools, and programs throughout the UCLA campus.

In response to the Moreno Report, the University of California Office of the President (UCOP) established the UC Senate-Administration Work Group on the Moreno Report, which issued their "Report to the President, Academic Council, and Chancellors" in late December 2013. Their report stated, "Systemwide P&T [Promotion and Tenure] has been concerned about *low level discriminatory actions* that occur over a long period of time—things such as undervaluation, *microaggression*, and *marginalization*—that never as a single instance reach the threshold for filing a formal grievance" (UC Senate-Administration Work Group 2013, 10; emphasis mine). One of the UCOP responses was to initiate a UC system-wide seminar for university leaders at each of the ten UC campuses. The seminar was entitled "Fostering Inclusive Excellence: Strategies and Tools for Department Chairs and Deans." The goals of the four-hour seminar were to: (1) help participants gain a better understanding of implicit bias and *microaggressions* and their impact on departmental/school climate; (2) increase participants' effectiveness at recognizing and interrupting/addressing *microaggressions* when they occur; and (3) discuss tools and strategies for developing an inclusive departmental/school climate (UC Office of the President 2015; emphasis mine). I was asked to give a seminar lecture entitled "Using the Critical Race Tools of Racial and Gender Microaggressions to Examine Everyday Racism in Academic Spaces."[6] The seminar took place on each of the ten UC campuses for department chairs, deans, and other campus senior leadership throughout the 2014–2015 academic year.

In the three years since the Moreno Report, I have given over seventy public lectures, presentations, and workshops on racial microaggressions at my university and other public and private universities, and in other professional and community settings. I have spoken to high school, undergraduate, graduate, and professional students from various departments and schools, teachers and teacher candidates, principals and principal candidates, counselors, university leaders, and civic leaders. While the work has a research and theoretical foundation, I have tried to speak to policy and activist audiences—people who can use the tool of racial microaggressions to bring about social change in their policy and activist spaces—in order to give voice and tools to people who serve those at the margins of society.

What Have I Learned?

In the twenty-three years that I've worked in the field of racial microaggressions, I have researched, published, and spoken on the importance of this concept and what we need to do to move the field forward to improve the lives of those who experience this form of everyday racism. I would like to share five things that have affected the way I view racial microaggressions and why this tool is important to the public discourse on race and racism in and out of higher education.

1. The *micro* in microaggressions does not mean "less than." Rather, the micro in microaggressions means "in the everyday."
2. The impact of verbal and non-verbal racial microaggressive assaults on people of color in the everyday is cumulative.
3. Racial microaggressions matter because they are symptoms of larger structural problems—racism and white supremacy.
4. We need to acknowledge and disrupt the discourses of racial micro-aggressions in the everyday.
5. People of color need to validate and affirm dignity and humanity, and support one another as a response to racial microaggressions.

Research in higher education has identified not only the academic constraints but also the physiological and psychological consequences caused by racial microaggressions over time. Research has also shown that people of color respond to racial microaggressions in powerful ways that counter negative perceptions and stereotypes based on race, gender, class, language, sexuality, immigration status, phenotype, accent, and surname. The analytical tool of racial microaggressions seeks to give people of color who experience this form of everyday racism a "name for their pain." In doing so, researchers and educators are also given tools to expose, challenge, and transform educational spaces to be more inclusive of a diversity that values the presence, knowledge, history and humanity of students of color—those at the academic and social margins.

This is what racial microaggressions are, why they matter, and why I do this work.

NOTES

1. These quotes represent the Jesuit philosophy of service to others, and specifically to the poor, that I experienced as an undergraduate and graduate student at Loyola University of Los Angeles in the late 1960s and 1970s.

2. See Pierce (1969; 1970).

3. I now define racial microaggressions as one form of systemic everyday racism used to keep those at the racial margins in their place. Racial microaggressions are verbal and non-verbal assaults directed toward people of color, often carried out in subtle, automatic, or unconscious forms. They are layered assaults, based on a person of color's race, gender, class, sexuality, language, immigration status, phenotype, accent, or surname. They are cumulative assaults that take a physiological, psychological, and academic toll on people of color.

4. In one of the most comprehensive histories of racial microaggressions, Wong et al. (2014) state that the Solorzano, Ceja, and Yosso (2000) article was the first empirical article published on racial microaggressions since Chester Pierce's earlier work. Indeed, my article on Chicana and Chicano scholars (Solorzano 1998) was published two years earlier. Also, my 1997 article on racial stereotyping is my first to conceptualize critical race theory and racial microaggressions within teacher education (see Solorzano 1997).

5. The *Grutter* case went to the US Supreme Court and as of this writing remains the legal precedent for the use of race as one element in the admissions process.

6. My colleague Lindsay Perez Huber, from California State University, Long Beach, gave five of the ten UCOP lectures on racial microaggressions.

REFERENCES

Allen, Walter R., and Daniel Solorzano. 2001. "Affirmative action, educational equity and campus racial climate: A case study of the University of Michigan Law School." *UC Berkeley La Raza Law Journal* 12: 237–363.

Davis, Peggy. 1989. "Law as microaggression." *Yale Law Journal* 98: 1559–77.

Kohli, Rita, and Daniel Solorzano. 2012. "Teachers, please learn our names!: Racial microaggressions and the K–12 classroom." *Race, Ethnicity, and Education* 15: 441–62.

Ledesma, Maria, and Daniel Solorzano. 2013. "Naming their pain: How everyday microaggressions impact students and teachers." In *Contesting the myth of a "post racial" era: The continued significance of race in US education,* edited by Dorinda J. Carter Andrews and Franklin Tuitt, 112–27, New York: Peter Lang.

Moreno, Carlos, Maga Jackson-Triche, Gary Nash, Constance Rice, and Bob Suzuki. 2013. "Independent investigative report on acts of bias and discrimination involving faculty at the University of California, Los Angeles." Los Angeles: UCLA Office of the Chancellor.

Perez Huber, Lindsay, and Daniel Solorzano. 2015a. "Visualizing everyday racism: Critical race theory, visual microaggressions, and the historical image of Mexican banditry." *Qualitative Inquiry* 21: 223–38.

Perez Huber, Lindsay, and Daniel Solorzano. 2015b. "Racial microaggressions as a tool for critical race research." *Race, Ethnicity, and Education* 18: 297–320.

Perez Huber, Lindsay, and Daniel Solorzano. 2015c. "Racial microaggressions: What they are, what they are not, and why they matter." *Latino Policy & Issues Brief No. 30.* Los Angeles: UCLA Chicano Studies Research Center.

Perez Huber, Lindsay, and Daniel Solorzano. In press. "Teaching racial microaggressions: Implications of critical race hypos for social work." *Journal of Ethnic & Cultural Diversity in Social Work.*

Pierce, Chester. 1969. "Is bigotry the basis of the medical problem of the ghetto?" In *Medicine in the ghetto,* edited by J. C. Norman, 301–14. New York: Meredith Corporation.

Pierce, Chester. 1970. "Offensive mechanisms." In *The Black seventies,* edited by Floyd Barbour, 265–82. Boston, MA: Porter Sargent.

Pierce, Chester, J. Carew, D. Pierce-Gonzalez, and D. Wills. 1978. "An experiment in racism: TV commercials." In *Television and education,* edited by Chester Pierce, 62–88. Beverly Hills, CA: Sage,.

Smith, William, Tara Yosso, and Daniel Solorzano. 2006. "Challenging racial battle fatigue on historically white campuses: A critical race examination of race-related stress." In *Faculty of color teaching in predominantly white colleges and universities,* edited by Christine Stanley, 299–327. Bolton, MA: Anker Publishing.

Solorzano, Daniel. 1997. "Images and words that wound: Critical race theory, racial stereotyping, and teacher education." *Teacher Education Quarterly*, 24: 5–19.

Solorzano, Daniel. 1998. "Critical race theory, racial and gender microaggressions, and the experiences of Chicana and Chicano scholars." *International Journal of Qualitative Studies in Education* 11: 121–36.

Solorzano, Daniel, Walter Allen, and Grace Carroll. 2002. "Keeping race in place: A case study of racial microaggressions and campus racial climate at the University of California, Berkeley." *UCLA Chicano/Latino Law Review* 23: 15–111.

Solorzano, Daniel, Miguel Ceja, and Tara Yosso. 2000. "Critical race theory, racial microaggressions and campus racial climate: The experiences of African American college students." *Journal of Negro Education* 69: 60–73.

Solorzano, Daniel, and Lindsay Perez Huber. 2012. "Microaggressions, racial." In *Encyclopedia of diversity in education*, edited by James Banks, 1489–92. Thousand Oaks, CA: Sage Publications.

Torres, Carlos. 1998. *First Freire: Early writings in social justice education.* New York: Teachers College Press.

UC Office of the President. 2015. "Fostering inclusive excellence: Strategies and tools for department chairs and deans." Oakland: University of California Office of the President.

UC Senate–Administration Work Group on the Moreno Report. 2013. "Report to the president, academic council, and chancellors." Oakland: University of California Office of the President.

Wong, Gloria, Annie O. Derthick, E. David, Anne Saw, and Sumie Okazaki. 2014. "The what, the why, and the how: A review of racial microaggressions research in psychology." *Race and Social Problems* 6: 181–200.

Yosso, Tara, Miguel Ceja, Wesley Smith, and Daniel Solorzano. 2009. "Critical race theory, racial microaggressions, and campus racial climate For Latina/o undergraduates." *Harvard Educational Review* 79: 659–90.

chapter 14

A Road Less Traveled

The Responsibilities of the Intellectual

WILLIAM G. TIERNEY

The challenge of learning more about my research areas of inquiry and writing texts of consequence remains the centerpiece of my intellectual life. I have found, in some respects, that putting pen to paper gets harder, not easier, as I have matured. Over the course of my academic career perhaps the greatest lesson I have learned is how little I know. Academics appear particularly susceptible to hubris, when humility is in order. As a graduate student, I wondered whether I would ever have anything to say since I knew so little. As an assistant professor, I feared that I did not know enough to earn tenure. And now, decades later, I still question whether what I write is well informed enough and of any consequence. Such caution is well deserved.

To know that one's understanding on a particular topic is incomplete does not absolve an individual from intellectual action. If I were only able to speak and write about an area of inquiry when I was certain, then I would likely say nothing. Thus, how one acts knowing that one's knowledge of a particular topic is imperfect and partial is a critical part of coming to terms with academic life.

An academic has multiple roads on which he or she may traverse. I do not disdain one or another avenue. I only know that I am reasonably content with the ones I have taken. Some colleagues, for example, will study one topic for much of their career. Others will write only for scholarly outlets, and still others will seek to affect the public through commentary on social media or in testimony at policy briefings. I do not believe that only one route exists for intellectual engagement, and in that light, I want each of us to be aware that we are choosing a particular path. I am troubled at times that a colleague may assume that only one choice is possible and that if another choice is made, then his or her colleague is gravely mistaken or morally failing. I am equally troubled by those who do not see their decisions as choices. By assuming that the choice one has made is the only possibility or not thinking through the array of possibilities that exist appears shortsighted to me, loaded with hubris and devoid of humility. What are the choices of which I speak? There are at least three.

Choosing How We Know What We Know

When I speak and write as a professor about my research, a degree of authority has been granted to me. I am circumspect in using that influence. For example, as a citizen I have very strong feelings about climate change, but I am not a scientist, and I have never done any research pertaining to the environment. Closer to my own area of inquiry, I know very little about early childhood education. I do not have the authority to speak as a professor about the climate or early childhood programs such as Head Start. The result is that I am careful about using my academic voice in research areas that are not my own.

I base how I use my authority on the work that I do and the evidence I accumulate. The tiresome debates about quantitative and qualitative research do not interest me very much in terms of choosing the sorts of topics that I ultimately may investigate or the data I might employ in proffering an opinion. I use as much data as I can amass before I write about a topic. I know that I am not speaking with certitude, but I also know I have gathered a great deal of evidence to corroborate what I am saying.

In this light, I am troubled by those whose epistemological framework is so rigid that they are prevented from speaking on any topic until the evidence is undeniable. I am equally troubled, if not more so, about those who, in a desire to be an advocate for a topic or a group, eschew standards of evidence and rush to judgment. I understand both positions. On the one hand often lies a positivist who seeks the scientific conditions of the laboratory to provide certainty about a particular social science dilemma. On the other hand lies a critical theorist who sees unjust structures and wishes to overthrow them based on particular assumptions about justice.

While my leanings are more toward critical theory, I also have come to learn that I neither advance my intellectual position nor help anyone if I am speaking without the necessary knowledge to proffer an informed opinion. Successful argumentation depends not on simply amassing probable evidence in support of a position, but on assembling as much data as possible to put forward a well-founded judgment. In my work, I am not simply trying to support what I believe to be true but instead trying to test various ideas, hunches, and hypotheses about why one or another proposition is plausible, even convincing.

In much of my recent work on college readiness, for example, I have called on quantitative studies of student course preparation and test-taking, and I have done life histories of individual students. I have used an understanding of race and inequity as a central organizing principle to form a plausible explanation for why so few students of color take Advanced Placement courses and/or graduate from high school and go on to a four-year university. I also have looked at the structural and bureaucratic shortcomings of college preparation programs that more often than not shortchange students on what is to be learned. I continue to investigate not merely the cognitive variables that students need upon entering college, but also the non-cognitive variables that I have come to define as "college knowledge." I have investigated the college-going culture of high schools with significant populations of low-income, first-generation students, as well as the climate those students face when they go to university.

The result is that I am able to write with reasonable confidence about the preparation of students, what they need to learn, why one or another program is not meeting specific needs, and what will occur when these students arrive at a two- or four-year institution. If I am able to speak with a degree of professorial authority, then the next question pertains to with whom I should speak.

Choosing For Whom to Write and with Whom to Speak

As a graduate student, I learned to write for one audience: scholars. The pace of publishing was unhurried. Months and years could go by before one's work was published. Such a leisurely pace afforded authors the opportunity to reflect on their work and adjust their writing in a thoughtful fashion.

Although scholarly work today occurs a bit more quickly, the pace remains relaxed compared to virtually every other means of communication. What has changed are the advances made in technology that have led to the demise of newspapers and the rise of social media. The result is that the number of audiences with whom a scholar might communicate has risen exponentially. Reporters from old media (e.g., newspapers, magazines) are still in search of authorities on a particular topic, but they have less time to work on a story. The result is that they need to speak with that authority in a more timely fashion than in the past. They also may be less versed on a topic, since reporters today tend to be more generalists than specialists. I try to offer immediate responses to requests, and I find myself giving mini-tutorials to reporters who may be neophytes with regard to the educational topic under investigation.

Social media also enable one to put forward his or her views in any number of outlets—Facebook, Instagram, blogs, the *Huffington Post*, and so on. Whereas a scholarly article may be 10,000 words, a tweet is 140 characters. The goal is to get ideas and opinions out in real time. The disadvantages, or cautions, are twofold. First, the desire to get a comment into the blogosphere immediately trumps the caution employed when one's colleagues review what gets to be published. Second, social media blend the personal with the professional. I might post an article about college readiness based on my research, and then my next three posts have to do with my personal interests: a restaurant I recently dined at, how the Dodgers are doing, and my concerns about ozone being released into the atmosphere.

An additional challenge is that writing thoughtful blog posts, op-eds, or articles for the general public is an entirely different skill than writing for one's colleagues. We usually do not teach graduate students or faculty how to write or make presentations. The consequence is that however much someone may wish to get his or her writing into the public sphere, it remains inaccessible to broad audiences.

Additional audiences that are relatively new for faculty include policymakers, venture capitalists, and philanthropists. Some individuals always have written grants to foundations, and others have testified before Congress. But graduate school largely does not prepare one for speaking to capitalists about an idea or to philanthropists about why they should endow one's institute. Moreover, in addition to congressional committees, a potpourri of think tanks has arisen, and they are anxious to tap into the knowledge base of faculty if the faculty members are able to communicate in a manner that is understandable to non-academics.

I have tried to work with many of these audiences, and it has taken a fair amount of energy, sort of like learning a new language. Op-eds in newspapers and the blog I maintained forced me to write in a different register. Conversations with philanthropists, venture capitalists, and editorial boards have helped me learn that what I think is important may not be of concern to them, or that I need to express my ideas in a different manner. I have made a choice, however, to try to reach these new audiences with the hope that my work can help bring about change.

This choice involves trade-offs and challenges. Communicating with these groups means that less time is available to attend to other groups. I do not generally encourage early career academics to spend a great deal of time writing blogs or communicating with non-academic audiences. As long as tenure remains wedded to traditional academic measures, graduate students and junior faculty should focus on traditional publishing outlets. Further, groups such as venture capitalists or foundation officers usually have very little interest in one's theoretical presuppositions. The ability to shift from one linguistic register to another when speaking with different groups, while also maintaining one's facility with traditional registers such as theory and method, is a challenge that needs to be mastered.

Choosing to Speak Truth to Power

I am able to utilize my voice to speak and write as a professor not only within the narrow confines of my research specialty, but also as an academic speaking on academic issues. Laura Perna (2016) has said that we should "ground our advocacy in research rather than opinion or anecdote" (331). I agree, but not all advocacy requires research. I am thinking here of academics who are silenced because their views are at odds with the government (Tierney and Postiglione 2015). In Egypt, a well-known sociologist, Saad Eddin Ibrahim, was arrested for his work, which was critical of Egyptian society. Abdul Sattar Jawad, a university dean and English professor, fled Iraq because of death threats as a result of the ideas he espoused. Abdolfattah Soltani is currently serving an eighteen-year prison sentence in Iran for establishing a human rights center. Gu Chuan was denied permission to leave China because of his blogging. In Turkey, hundreds of academics have been dismissed from their positions because they have opposed the government. At the University of Bahrain, Abdul Jalil Al-Singace, a professor of mechanical engineering, was sentenced to life in prison for his for pro-democracy activism.

These examples require me to raise my voice as an academic. When I am silent on such issues, I am failing in the role that has been accorded to me as a tenured professor (Tierney 2013). Indeed, I need to take such a point one step further. It is not particularly difficult to speak out against the imprisonment of a colleague in a country thousands of miles away. It simply takes believing that it is one of my responsibilities and educating myself about such issues.

It is harder to face the opprobrium of the university president by advocating a sit-in if the university does not enact a non-discrimination clause for

LGBTQ individuals. It is harder to be on the academic senate and tell the provost we should pause before establishing a branch campus in a country that does not allow academic freedom (Tierney and Lanford 2015). It is more difficult to tell your university's president that the janitorial staff is underpaid and deserve a living wage. And it is a challenge to confront one's dean, department chair, or colleague about comments that have short-circuited difficult dialogues about race, class, gender, or sexual orientation.

As I previously noted, early career faculty may hesitate to get involved in such issues because action involves risk. I can say that I took those risks, but I do not believe all of my younger colleagues need to follow in my footsteps. Those who are tenured have a different responsibility. Too many tenured faculty see tenure as a right. I see it as an obligation. Through tenure, I have been accorded an inordinate reward and privilege—a sinecure for life. Such freedom has placed on me three responsibilities. I have to marshal the best possible evidence to inform my research. I have to reach out to multiple audiences. And I have to initiate difficult dialogues that ensure that the academy remains a place where the search for truth is paramount.

REFERENCES

Perna, Laura W. 2016. "Throwing down the gauntlet: Ten ways to ensure that higher education research continues to matter." *Review of Higher Education* 39: 319–38.

Tierney, William G. 2013. "Beyond the ivory tower: The role of the intellectual in the 21st century." *Educational Researcher* 42: 295–303.

Tierney, William G., and Michael Lanford. 2015. "An investigation of the impact of international branch campuses on organizational culture." *Higher Education* 70: 283–98. doi: 10.1007/s10734-014-9845-7.

Tierney, William G., and Gerard Postiglione. 2015. "Integrity at Risk." *South China Morning Post*, July 5.

chapter 15

Using Philosophy to Develop a Thoughtful Approach to Going Public or Not

ADRIANNA KEZAR

For me, research ethics and public engagement are a matter of philosophy. I have conducted in-depth readings and reflections on my role as a researcher, the role of research in the world, and our ethical obligations as researchers. In this essay, I bring up my own research occasionally as examples, but I foreground philosophical views over personal choices and experience.

For me, public engagement is a responsibility of scholars and part of quality scholarship. We as scholars have a responsibility to inform public debates on key policy and practice issues that affect education. It is not enough to simply produce research; we must bring that research to forums where the public good is debated. My engagement includes writing for practitioner audiences (via articles for *Change*, *About Campus*, *Academe*, *The Presidency*, *Liberal Education*, etc.), partnering with national associations and groups (e.g., Delphi Project on Changing Faculty and Student Success), participating in activism and service on my own campus and in the community, working to shape state and federal policy, consulting, training, engaging the media, conducting community-based research, and providing national leadership (e.g., as an accreditation commissioner).

I consider what I do "public scholarship" in service of a diverse democracy and social justice. Democracy is stronger when it includes all voices—particularly minority and marginalized voices based on class, caste, creed, religion, ethnicity, gender, sexual orientation, age, disability, geographical isolation, socioeconomic status, and other characteristics of difference. Public scholarship should work with as many stakeholders as possible and reach out to less powerful and minority voices, which are often not engaged through our research.

By social justice, I mean promoting a just society by challenging injustice. My studies explore ways to change higher education to be more equitable and better serve diverse students. Engagement should be mutual and two-way—not scholars telling practitioners what to do. Other forms of going public may be driven by other motivations. This is my own definition and approach.

How did I come to this view of engagement? Research paradigms developed over the last several centuries have helped to codify philosophical discussions that address the questions posed in this very book (Kezar 2004). As a historian, I find that engaging with the historical dialogue on important topics is one of the best ways to develop informed and thoughtful choices. While I value the perspectives of my colleagues and try to learn from their experiences and my own, I also know that several centuries of debate and discussion offer a wise and complex perspective on the issues addressed in this book.

The role of personal experience in research, advocacy, research conflicts, and the notion of the public engagement is best informed by collective reflection by researchers within discourse communities (e.g., like-minded scholars). Researchers can come to very different and appropriate conclusions about the role of the researcher based on their perspective of research (Kezar 2006). There is not a single or best approach to public engagement. One scholar is not right and another wrong for having different ways of utilizing personal experience or deciding to act as an advocate or not. Research paradigms offer a community of individuals who have thought through these issues and developed a linked set of logic related to these important questions as well as advice about how to engage in research in ethical ways. What I hope to demonstrate in this essay is the value that scholars can gain from engaging with philosophical inquiry into these issues and joining discourse communities that examine the obligations of researchers as part of their research.

Research Paradigms and the Role of the Researcher

In this short essay, I cannot review the wisdom of the last several thousand years. Instead, I present table 1 to summarize key ideas that have emerged across different research paradigms: post-positivist, constructivist, critical, and participatory (Kezar 2004, 2006). Denzin and Lincoln (1994) outline core differences in these paradigms around ontology, epistemology, axiology, and methodology.

Here I focus on values and ethics in research. For example, post-positivists tend to see their main goal as describing and predicting the future based on an understanding of underlying mechanisms that shape a known reality. In

TABLE 1

Some axiological positions of selected research paradigms

	Positivist paradigm	Interpretive paradigm	Critical paradigm	Participatory paradigm
Goals	To explain, predict, and control	To develop understanding; reconstruction	To critique and transform	To create changes in the social world through mutual engagement and learning
Role of researcher	Neutral or objective	Subjective: involved in the social world; understanding comes from interaction	Intersubjective: involved in the social world, but understanding comes from stepping back from daily experience to see larger patterns	Subjective: understanding comes from interaction in the social world; interested in affecting and changing the social world
Advocacy	Being an advocate would threaten knowledge development and potentially create bias	Scholar develops relationships through research that must be negotiated in order to stay true to the understanding developed.	Scholar has an ethical obligation to advocate for oppressed or marginalized groups	Scholar has an obligation to work to create changes, which may involve advocacy
Relationship to the public	Important for researcher to stay unbiased and distant from objects of study	Uncommitted to interaction with the public as having either a value or bias	Important to interact with the public in order to change power dynamics	Important to interact with the public to change policy and practice through mutual learning and knowledge development
Values and personal views of researcher	Excluded	Included, but careful not to impose on findings or participants	Included	Included

this view, researchers are assumed to do their best work when they are neutral or objective. In contrast, researchers from a critical perspective see their goal as shedding light on power structures, questioning current practices, and advocating for changes that would lead to greater equality and social justice.

The role of the researcher is seen quite differently in the two traditions. Post-positivists, influenced by Enlightenment notions of rationality and leery of dogmas, typically believe that personal experience can create forms of bias in interpreting data, that possessing certain value stances can alter the ability of researchers to see data sources impartially, and that researchers should have no connection or relationship to groups or individuals that may sway their interpretations of data. Researchers from a critical paradigm, however, believe that personal experience provides insight, values, and interests that inform the research process.

Some paradigms see public engagement as inherent to the research process. The participatory paradigm can only achieve its goal of change through engagement with the public in a process of mutual learning. An understanding of the different paradigms allows researchers to respect differences in approach and appreciate the different grounds by which they make decisions about their research approaches and ethics.

Although most researchers are embedded in a single research paradigm, increasingly researchers are developing arguments for combining the assumptions of more than one paradigm. For example, I have utilized assumptions from critical and constructivist paradigms throughout my career to inform my research. While these paradigm categories sometimes hide their potential overlap, they offer an understanding of the connected logic that has driven research communities, often implicitly, over time. Moreover, there are ethical stances in paradigms that cannot be reconciled or combined. Although combining is possible, researchers must examine the commensurability of stances. Making the assumptions within these paradigms explicit forces researchers to engage in important questioning and to reflect on fundamental questions of how researchers do their work—the very purpose of this volume.

In addition to understanding the general paradigm frames of reference, it is important to engage specific philosophical traditions and scholars within these broad paradigms to guide our work. Broad categories do not always provide the details of particular philosophical streams. For example, feminist scholars within critical theory offer a wealth of perspective on research ethics (Miller et al. 2012).

While I have engaged many specific philosophers, one theorist whom I will highlight in this essay is Jürgen Habermas, a critical theorist whose work on communicative action speaks directly to the issues of the role of the researcher and engaging publics in our research. Given his direct attention to engaging the public and creating democratic discourse, Habermas is one of the most relevant and well-regarded scholars on the topic. While general paradigms are helpful, attention to particular thinkers provides more precise arguments and perspective.

Goals, Role of the Researcher, and Advocacy

Critical constructivism drives my research and informs my perspective. Reflecting a critical and constructivist perspective, in my research I try to understand and critique existing power structures and assumed ways of practice that might hide privilege or mask racism, sexism, and other forms of inequality and discrimination. As a constructivist, I want to do more than question and identify power structures that create inequalities. I want to help create new structures and cultures based on social justice.

In critical traditions, the researcher is assumed to be an advocate. I have always considered myself to be an advocate in whatever research I am conducting. Currently, I am engaged in research for the purpose of advocating for new practices within the academy. When I conducted research on leadership, I saw myself as an advocate for more egalitarian forms of leadership that could shatter hierarchical and unequal forms of power within organizations. In my research on adjunct faculty, I have considered myself an advocate for a group that has experienced marginalization and oppressive working conditions, with fast-food-worker pay levels, no benefits, and no job security. As I have conducted research on change and transformation in the academy, I have identified and worked to progress changes that will create a more socially just academy, including equity/diversity initiatives, service learning, collaborative learning, learning communities, and other forms of non-hierarchical learning, as well as programs and services aimed at altering the academy to make it a more inclusive environment for first-generation, underrepresented, and low-income students. I have always seen myself as an advocate for reforms that are aimed at a more socially just vision of the academic enterprise and not simply a researcher of programs and initiatives.

In drawing on Habermas (1985), I have found it important as a critical theorist to not speak exclusively to other academics, but to engage the public around these important areas of research. Habermas describes the role of academics in working to create democratic spaces for conversations about the ideas that academics are researching. He notes the importance of interactions with the public directed toward mutual understanding, rather than being coercive or manipulative. As I work to initiate more service learning, I am actively engaged with understanding the perspectives of those who do not see the value of this approach or community agencies that often feel they are used by elite institutions to further their educational goals while downplaying community development. Habermas's work provides a foundation for how I can achieve this goal of engaging and interacting with important publics that are affected by my research, hearing new voices, and altering my perspective. Habermas's work outlines the ethical obligations of academics to engage the public, ways to conduct this public interaction, and goals for such interactions. Moreover, he outlines a set of procedures for developing these mutual types of communication experiences. One begins by identifying the publics who might be affected by the research, being as inclusive as possible. Various publics may question any assertion or part of the research.

One problematic issue that emerges in engaging publics is the unequal power of different stakeholders in our research. How do you ensure voice for less powerful publics in "democratic spaces"? Habermas wrestled with this issue, but I am not fully satisfied with his conclusions (as are other critics). This remains a troubling area for researchers who want to promote public scholarship and engage publics with unequal levels of power. The participatory and critical paradigms suggest beginning with and weighing more heavily the voices of those who have been marginalized.

The Role of Personal Experience

Within the critical and constructivist paradigms, my personal experiences are assumed to affect my research work. A researcher is not an objective or neutral observer, but rather understands that politics and power are ever present. An important methodological practice within the constructivist paradigm is to deeply understand the ways that personal experience may influence your research by creating bias or advancing understanding. In addition, it is important at times to bracket out one's understanding to look at situations with fresh eyes. Because we are so ingrained in our culture, we often misunderstand the nature of existence and experience. Personal experiences and perspective are carefully explored as a part of the research process. Different forms of qualitative research speak to making explicit one's personal experience. In phenomenology a researcher journals experiences in order to bracket them while reviewing the data. To see beyond existing assumptions, we often have to push aside our current understandings. Research paradigms provide key information about how to thoughtfully utilize and navigate our own personal experiences when conducting research. In the critical paradigm, personal experience with oppression and marginalization can provide special insight. For example, people of color and women may possess a better understanding of racism and sexism. Therefore, personal experience can lend credibility to research.

Habermas (1985) also acknowledges the role of our own experience in the research process. He was very clear that our personal experience should not be allowed to dominate; part of our goal in interacting with the public is to reshape and refashion our understanding. If a researcher engages the public and does not have a changed perspective, then he or she is likely not authentically and mutually engaging with the publics that inform the research. This view also suggests that our personal experience can be a touchstone but should not be the driving force in our work.

Public Intellectuals and Going Public

Within critical theory, being a public intellectual is a way to challenge dominant forms of knowledge that are embedded in the media and various public dialogues. Habermas (1985) suggests the importance of dialogue, through which the public has an opportunity to inform our research and is engaged deeply and meaningfully. The public intellectual is typically conceived as a one-way communicator aimed at persuading the public. Habermas's work challenges us to consider more mutual ways to engage the public.

In my work on non-tenure-track faculty, constant interactions with various publics have reshaped my understanding and helped me incorporate diverse views. My interaction with different types of adjuncts helped me understand the challenge of universal policies, and my conversations with different institutional leaders helped me better understand how local contexts shape working conditions. If I had gone public with data that were based on academic research or my own perspective, or that were provided by advocacy organizations for non-tenure track faculty, I would have missed pivotal information for creating wiser, more appropriate, and more ethical policy. Developing an understanding that is informed by as many voices as possible achieves Habermas's hope of creating more democratic forms of understanding. Free, open, mutual communication is at the center of Habermas's theory of communicative action and public scholarship.

My greatest concern with the notion of the public intellectual is that it too narrowly defines the role of public engagement. I encourage scholars to consider a broader notion of public scholarship, embedded in Habermas's vision (as well as the vision of others, such as John Dewey). Public engagement should extend beyond the media—where public intellectuals typically aim—to involve various publics, including those who are the beneficiaries of or agents within the research and those who will act on the research to develop policy and shape practice. The public should be considered in an inclusive way—encompassing students and parents, the media, the general public, and, particularly, groups that may have formerly had no access to our research or have been excluded as an audience. Public scholarship asks us to consider the ways that we can reach out and mutually engage the public with our research—in its creation, dissemination, and application. It reflects more participatory action research. Current versions of the public intellectual have been usurped and embedded with neoliberal notions of visibility, prestige seeking, and revenue generation for the individual and the institution in which they are embedded. This appropriation of the public intellectual by neoliberalism is worrying, as the focus is more on the benefits to scholars than for the publics they are meant to serve.

I hope I have intrigued you to use the scholarship from research paradigms and philosophy to inform your views of research ethics. I also encourage you to read the other essays in this volume with these research paradigms in mind. Many researchers are not explicit about their paradigms, but rather tacitly adopt research values through graduate school socialization and early interaction with colleagues. I invite you to more explicitly choose your ethical obligations. These are some of the most important choices you will make.

REFERENCES

Denzin, Norman., and Yvonna Lincoln. 1994. *Handbook of qualitative research.* Thousand Oaks, CA: Sage.

Habermas, Jürgen. 1985. *The theory of communicative action, vol. 2: Lifeworld and system: A critique of functionalist reason,* Boston, MA: Beacon Press.

Kezar, Adrianna J. 2004. "Wrestling with philosophy: Improving scholarship in higher education." *Journal of Higher Education* 75: 42–55.

Kezar, Adrianna J. 2006. "To develop or not to develop theory: That is the question?" In *Higher education: Handbook of theory and research*, vol. 21, edited by John C. Smart, 283–344. New York, NY: Springer.

Miller, Tina, Maxine Birch, Melanie Mauthner, and Julie Jessop, eds. 2012. *Ethics in qualitative research.* Thousand Oaks, CA: Sage.

chapter 16

Research for Policy in Higher Education

The Case for Research–Practice Partnerships

ADAM GAMORAN

Today, higher education is being challenged from all sides. Access, completion, cost, debt, and alternatives to traditional modes of higher education are all identified as issues that demand response. While research studies are emerging in reaction to each of these challenges, all too often decisions are made (or resisted) without regard to the research findings. This is a familiar story in the policy world. How can we change the narrative in higher education?

The William T. Grant Foundation, which I lead, has a long history of supporting research intended to inform policy and practice. More than a quarter of a century ago, we released *The Forgotten Half: Pathways to Success for America's Youth and Young Families* (William T. Grant Foundation Commission on Work, Family, and Citizenship 1988; Halpern 1998), which decried our national underinvestment in youth who do not attend college and led to a variety of efforts to improve the transition of youth to adult society. More recently, a new report, *The New Forgotten Half and Research Directions to Support Them* (Rosenbaum et al. 2015), identified today's challenge as supporting young people who attend college but fail to earn a degree or certification, or who transfer. This report, too, is intended to point the way toward new policy directions and spark new research to address unanswered questions.

While the foundation has long been concerned with pressing policy issues, the specific questions our grantees have addressed have changed over time as new social issues emerge. Early in 2014 we launched our latest focus to support research on reducing inequality among young people. Higher education is an area of principal concern, and we commissioned the *The New Forgotten*

Half to emphasize our interest in this domain. Yet the challenge of seeing research move from academic articles to policy decisions remains as vexing in this area as in any other.

Recognizing the challenge of linking research and policy, the foundation also supports studies aimed at improving the use of research evidence in policy and practice. Here the goal is to go beyond exhorting researchers to conduct research that has use value, to supporting a portfolio of scholarship that will develop new understandings of how to increase the usefulness—and use—of research evidence. When the foundation began nearly a decade ago to focus on how research evidence was used, it did so in the context of a powerful current of ideas focused on the need to improve the quality of research evidence (William T. Grant Foundation 2016). If only the evidence were more rigorous, the thinking went, it would be worthy of greater attention from policymakers and thus be more influential. Foundation staff were skeptical that increased rigor would lead to greater use and subsequently funded a line of research to increase understanding of the barriers to and supports for the use of research evidence. A substantial portion of this work was undertaken in education, focused largely on the elementary and secondary levels (Finnigan and Daly 2014). These studies showed that the quality of evidence was not the primary driver of its use. Instead, the use of research evidence in decision making was more related to the quality of relationships between the producers and consumers of evidence, as well as the intermediaries who knit them together (Tseng and Nutley 2014). Decision makers are more likely to draw on evidence from sources they trust (Asen 2014, 2015), which means that evidence producers or intermediaries need to establish trusting relationships to improve the prospects that the evidence they convey will inform decisions. To complete the cycle of evidence production and use, trusting relationships need to be supported by sustainable structures, and researchers need incentives to ask the sorts of questions whose answers will add value to the deliberations of decision makers. Not only does research evidence need to be timely, relevant, rigorous, and accessible, but it also needs to be conveyed through relationships of trust that give decision makers the confidence to rely upon it (Steuerle and Jackson 2016; Tseng and Nutley 2014).

Research–Practice Partnerships in Education

In K–12 education, research–practice partnerships are emerging in cities across the nation to provide the sort of structures that can sustain the relationships needed to get potentially useful evidence actually used (Coburn and Penuel 2016; Coburn, Penuel, and Geil 2013). For example, the Consortium on Chicago School Research recently celebrated its twenty-fifth anniversary of serving as a bridge between the school district and research community to inform and assess policy and practice in the Chicago public schools. Researchers and district staff work together to identify problems whose research-based solutions may help shape district policy. With the cooperation of the district, including access to administrative data, university-based researchers undertake studies that respond to the identified problems. For instance, concerns about high rates of high school dropouts led consortium researchers to identify early predictors of dropping out (Allensworth and Easton 2005, 2007). The research findings led to an early warning system that was straightforward to implement and helps the district provide services to students who need them before they reach the point of dropping out. The collaborative research on early warnings is an especially powerful example because it not only influenced school district policy in Chicago, but also served as a national model.[1]

Since the Chicago consortium was created in 1990, many other K–12 partnerships have formed in cities, including New York, Baltimore, Los Angeles, Houston, New Orleans, and elsewhere. In addition, the National Network of Education Research–Practice Partnerships, formed in 2015, lists twenty-two members.[2] Writing about the Houston Education Research Consortium, Turley and Stevens (2015) argued that partnerships between school districts and universities carry benefits for both sides. For school districts, the partnerships expand their capacity to examine their own data, elevate the importance of research as a tool for addressing district challenges, and provide a trusted but independent voice on district programs and policies. For universities, the partnerships lead researchers to work on problems that really matter, allow access to administrative data that speak meaningfully to the research questions, make researchers more competitive for research funding, and enable universities to serve their mission of community engagement. The national network encourages the formation of new partnerships, builds knowledge across districts by generating comparative research and synthesizing findings, and collectively pursues policy reforms.[3]

Research–Practice Partnerships at the Postsecondary Level

These K–12 partnerships may serve as models for collaborative endeavors that could be established at the postsecondary level. Like school districts, universities collect large amounts of institutional data that are rarely fully tapped. A postsecondary partnership model would rest on a shared commitment to make institutional data available to test out various policies aimed at addressing a common problem. Although institutional research offices may have more capacity than school district research offices, they are like school districts in that the pressure to address day-to-day administrative questions and compliance demands makes it difficult to undertake long-term studies directed at broader questions of policy and practice. A consortium of higher education institutions working with a trusted university partner could provide a conducive context for undertaking research whose findings will aid policy at the national, state, and institutional levels.

In contrast to most K–12 partnerships, a higher education research–practice partnership is unlikely to be confined to a single city, since that is not how universities are organized. Instead, such a partnership is more likely to have a state, regional, or thematic focus. For example, public institutions in a state might form a partnership with researchers at a flagship university; or institutions in different regions focused on a common problem, such as reducing completion gaps for underrepresented demographic groups, might partner with a research center devoted to that challenge. A less centralized model might feature multiple institutions, each with research and policy staff focused on a coherent challenge and sharing methods and findings. By sustaining relationships between researchers and practitioners over time, the partnerships would be able to take on long-term research agendas that can be realized through a series of studies.

The promise of a postsecondary research–practice partnership depends on the commitment of individual researchers to listen to their institutional partners about the challenges they face. Describing the difficulty of developing trust in K–12 partnerships, Turley and Stevens (2015) explained that such relationships "do not occur naturally or immediately but require a significant investment of time and effort" (10S). Until trust is established, connections across organizations are tenuous, and developing trust requires persistent communication and a willingness to learn from individuals in the partner organization. Individuals from each side need to be involved in crafting the mission of the partnership, which must reflect the perspectives of both organizations. Whereas researchers bring methodological and substantive expertise, institutional partners are intimately familiar with the practical challenges of their work. Researchers must remain open to understanding these challenges and applying their skills to addressing questions whose answers matter in the practical context (Coburn et al. 2013).

Examples of Postsecondary Research–Practice Partnerships

Two examples illustrate the potential for research–practice partnerships at the postsecondary level. One involves research universities and the other is based in community colleges.

CIRTL

The Center for the Integration of Research, Teaching, and Learning (CIRTL) provides an existing model of a postsecondary research–practice partnership.[4] CIRTL is a national network of research universities focused on improving undergraduate instruction in the STEM (science, technology, engineering, and mathematics) fields by preparing graduate students to be effective teachers before they advance to their faculty positions. Now in its eleventh year, the CIRTL network includes forty-five universities in the United States and one in Canada. Three core ideas guide CIRTL's work: (1) teaching-as-research, which is the notion that STEM instructors can systematically study their own teaching as a way to improve it; (2) learning communities, which bring together groups of faculty, staff, and students to generate and share knowledge about effective teaching; and (3) learning-through-diversity, which draws on the varied backgrounds of faculty and students to enhance the undergraduate learning experience of all. CIRTL's member institutions develop and share an array of learning events, such as workshops and webcasts, that convey research findings to the rest of the network. The network has also developed a massive open online course (MOOC) that introduces current and future faculty to evidence-based teaching practices.[5]

As a model, CIRTL has similarities and differences with the K–12 education research–practice partnerships. As at the K–12 level, CIRTL strives to create a normative environment in which research evidence plays a role in shaping policy and practice. In addition, CIRTL researchers are incentivized to carry out studies whose findings have direct bearing on decisions about instruction. In contrast to the K–12 partnerships, however, CIRTL research is often carried out by the practitioners themselves, who are typically researchers with PhDs (though few are trained in social science methods). This has the great advantage of eliminating the need to bridge between research and practice (since the researcher and practitioner are one and the same), but the disadvantage of relatively small scale, which constrains the design of research and the conclusions that may be derived.

Carnegie Math Pathways

Another partnership model at the postsecondary level involves community colleges in a networked improvement community (NIC), a partnership model that establishes patterns of collaboration both within and across institutions to improve practice in a particular domain (Bryk, Gomez, and Grunow 2011; Bryk et al. 2015). Carnegie Math Pathways addresses the problem of low rates of success in remedial or "developmental" math in community colleges, which poses barriers to students wishing to pursue the credits needed to complete prerequisites, qualify for transfer programs, or earn a degree.[6] The challenge of low success rates is especially prevalent among students from low-income and minority backgrounds (Bailey and Cho 2010). Carnegie features two pathways to success: Quantway, a one-semester course that emphasizes quantitative reasoning, and Statway, a year-long course that focuses on statistics, data analysis, and causal reasoning. Both courses introduce students to the usual content of developmental math courses but in ways that are more accessible and engaging for students than the typical lecture and exercise format.

The researchers and institutional actors who partner together in a NIC set common, measurable targets and examine data to gauge success toward reaching those targets (Bryk et al. 2011). They use common tools, such as conceptual maps to guide instructional design and peer-to-peer technologies, to carry out continuous improvement efforts. They share findings and continuously refine their approaches in pursuit of greater success (Bryk et al. 2015). In Carnegie Math Pathways, university-based researchers collaborate with community college faculty and administrators to foster improvement (Yamada and Bryk 2015).

With forty-nine community colleges in fourteen states, Carnegie Math Pathways is the nation's most extensive postsecondary NIC.[7] A recent cross-site study of Statway yielded remarkable evidence of success: around 55 percent of students enrolled in Statway earned college math credit, compared with 14 to 18 percent of students in a matched comparison group of students enrolled in developmental math for up to three years (Yamada and Bryk 2016). The findings held across participating colleges and racial and ethnic subgroups, and the contrast was greatest for students who were least well prepared in prior mathematics.

Key Features of Postsecondary Research–Practice Partnerships

One aspect of both CIRTL and Carnegie Math Pathways that distinguishes them from most K–12 research–practice partnerships is their focus on a coherent problem (improving undergraduate STEM teaching for the former, and increasing success rates in developmental math for the latter). By contrast, K–12 research–practice partnerships are commonly more comprehensive and flexible, addressing a wider range of challenges that arise in their distinctive policy contexts. Future postsecondary partnerships might adopt the models represented by CIRTL or by Carnegie Math Pathways to focus on specific challenges, or they might be structured more like their K–12 counterparts. For example, public universities in a single state or region might collaborate with a research center stocked with social scientists who would undertake studies of a wide range of policies regarding some of the most challenging issues of the present, such as access, completion, and modes of instruction. These partnerships would have enough scope to allow large-scale comparative designs that could enable at least tentative conclusions about the effectiveness of different approaches undertaken at the different partner universities. Consider, for example, a consortium of universities committed to studying the potential of different types of instructional delivery systems, such as traditional classroom lectures, flipped classrooms, fully online courses, and blended approaches, to reduce gaps in course success rates. A cross-university comparative study carried out by scholars skilled in social science methods, drawing on administrative data to monitor students' progress over time, could yield more powerful conclusions than those of a single instructor, department, or university. These findings would be relevant not only for the participating universities but also for universities across the country.

Whatever model is adopted, research–practice partnerships at the postsecondary level would share at least three key features. First, they would build on long-term relationships that enable trust and facilitate sustained efforts over time to enact and study change. Second, the research agenda would be co-constructed by researchers and practitioners so that the questions addressed in research would be those whose answers could guide policy and practice. Third, the partnerships would facilitate sharing of institutional data so that researchers can aid decision makers in understanding the consequences of their actions and the potential for innovation. Each of these features calls on researchers to be open to new directions for their research to increase its value in a practical context. But they also afford new opportunities for scholarship that might otherwise remain closed.

Funding Research–Practice Partnerships

How might research–practice partnerships in postsecondary education be funded and sustained? Few enterprises will have the resources available to CIRTL, which was established with a $10 million grant from the National Science Foundation (NSF) to the Wisconsin Center for Education Research at the University of Wisconsin–Madison, in an NSF competition to fund research centers of learning and teaching.[8] Carnegie Math Pathways is an initiative of the Carnegie Foundation for the Advancement of Teaching, which is supported by an array of public and private funders. Future partnerships that, like these examples, are directed at specific challenges may find funding from public or private sources that are centrally concerned with those particular challenges. Geographically organized partnerships aimed at the full range of higher education challenges, modeled after the K–12 partnerships, will probably need to rely on support from member institutions and perhaps from foundations that focus on higher education or particular geographic regions. Postsecondary partnerships of researchers, practitioners, and higher education decision makers are also likely to be in a strong position to compete for funding for specific research studies from national funders, including the postsecondary education research program at the US Department of Education's Institute of Sciences and a variety of private funders that have supported postsecondary education research, such as the Gates, Lumina, Spencer, and William T. Grant Foundations.

Research–practice partnerships are a demonstrated model for advancing research that matters to decision makers. Examples abound at the K–12 level, and at least two well-established and growing models exist at the postsecondary level. Creating new partnerships will take the commitment of institutions to provide a partnership infrastructure, commitment from researchers to address consequential questions, and commitment of those engaged in practice and policymaking to consider research evidence in their work. Incentives for institutions to participate include not only the chance to have their questions addressed and to collaborate with partner institutions that share similar concerns, but also the opportunity to bring in external resources, obtained competitively but from a position of strength afforded by the partnership. For addressing the manifold problems of higher education, research–practice partnerships are a promising way to bring research into the conversation.

ACKNOWLEDGMENTS

The author is grateful for helpful comments from Mark Connolly, Kim Dumont, Paul LeMahieu, Vivian Louie, Laura Perna, and Vivian Tseng.

NOTES

1. For more on the national diffusion of policies based on these findings, see http://consor tium.uchicago.edu/node/1168.

2. See http://nnerpp.rice.edu/.

3. Resources for research–practice partnerships are posted on the website of the William T. Grant Foundation (http://rpp.wtgrantfoundation.org).

4. More information on CIRTL may be found at http://www.cirtl.net/.

5. Information on the MOOC is posted at https://www.cirtl.net/p/cirtl-programming #MassiveOpenOnlineCourses(MOOCs).

6. Information on Carnegie Math Pathways is available at http://www.carnegiefoundation .org/in-action/carnegie-math-pathways/.

7. A list of institutions participating in Carnegie Math Pathways is posted at http://www .carnegiefoundation.org/in-action/carnegie-math-pathways/participating-institutions/.

8. For more on CIRTL's NSF award, see http://www.nsf.gov/awardsearch/showAward?AWD _ID=0227592. CIRTL's original grant was awarded January 1, 2003. I directed the Wisconsin Center for Education Research from 2004 to 2013, and the current director, Robert Mathieu, also directs the CIRTL network.

REFERENCES

Allensworth, Elaine, and John Q. Easton. 2005. *The on-track indicator as a predictor of high school graduation.* Chicago: Consortium on Chicago School Research.

Allensworth, Elaine, and John Q. Easton. 2007. *What matters for staying on-track and graduating in Chicago public high schools.* Chicago: Consortium on Chicago School Research.

Asen, Rob. 2014. *Trust and the use of research evidence.* New York: William T. Grant Foundation. http://wtgrantfoundation.org/trust-and-the-use-of-research-evidence.

Asen, Rob. 2015. *Democracy, deliberation, and education.* State College: Pennsylvania State University Press.

Bailey, Thomas, and Sung-Woo Cho. 2010. "Developmental education in community colleges." Issue brief. New York: Community College Research Center.

Bryk, Anthony S., Louis M. Gomez, and Alicia Grunow. 2011. "Getting ideas into action: Building networked improvement communities in education." In *Frontiers in sociology of education,* edited by M. T. Hallinan, 127–62. New York: Springer.

Bryk, Anthony S., Louis M. Gomez, Alicia Grunow, and Paul G. LeMahieu. 2015. *Learning to improve: How America's schools can get better at getting better.* Cambridge, MA: Harvard Education Press.

Coburn, Cynthia E., and William R. Penuel. 2016. "Research–practice partnerships in education: Outcomes, dynamics, and open questions." *Educational Researcher* 45: 48–54.

Coburn, Cynthia E., William R. Penuel, and Kimberly Geil. 2013. *Research-practice partnerships at the district level: A new strategy for leveraging research for educational improvement.* New York: William T. Grant Foundation. http://wtgrantfoundation.org/library/uploads/2015/10 /Research-Practice-Partnerships-at-the-District-Level.pdf.

Finnigan, Kara S., and Alan J. Daly, eds. 2014. *Using research evidence in education: From the schoolhouse door to Capitol Hill*. Heidelberg: Springer.

Halpern, Samuel, ed. 1998. *The forgotten half revisited: American youth and young families, 1988–2008*. Washington, DC: American Youth Policy Forum.

Rosenbaum, James, Caitlin Ahearn, Kelly Becker, and Janet Rosenbaum. 2015. *The new forgotten half and research directions to support them*. New York: William T. Grant Foundation.

Steuerle, Eugene, and Leigh Miles Jackson, eds. 2016. *Advancing the power of economic evidence to inform investments in children, youth, and families*. Washington, DC: National Academies Press.

Tseng, Vivian, and Sandra Nutley. 2014. "Building the infrastructure to improve the use and usefulness of research in education." In *Using research evidence in education: From the schoolhouse door to Capitol Hill*, edited by Kara S. Finnigan and Alan J. Daly, 163–75. Heidelberg: Springer.

Turley, Ruth N. López, and Carla Stevens. 2015. "Lessons from a school district-university research partnership: The Houston Education Research Consortium." *Educational Evaluation and Policy Analysis* 37: 6S–15S.

William T. Grant Foundation. 2016. *Improving the use of research evidence: An updated statement of research interests and applicant guidance*. New York: William T. Grant Foundation. http://wtgrantfoundation.org/library/uploads/2016/01/2016-URE-Supplemental-Guidance.pdf.

William T. Grant Foundation Commission on Work, Family, and Citizenship. 1988. *The forgotten half: Pathways to success for America's youth and young families*. New York: William T. Grant Foundation.

Yamada, Hiroyuki, and Anthony S. Bryk. 2016. "Assessing the first two years' effectiveness of Statway: A multilevel model with propensity score matching." *Community College Review* 44: 179–204.

chapter 17

Public Scholarship

Researchers Contributing to Equitable Diverse Democracies

JEANNIE OAKES AND ANTHONY A. BERRYMAN

Though our experience in connecting research, advocacy, and policy in higher education certainly varies, we share a fundamental belief in the centrality of equitable education for the health of a diverse democracy and a conviction that scholars have an *essential* obligation to shape educational systems in equitable ways. With decades of experience in higher education, Jeannie has aimed to provide technically solid evidence about prevailing inequities in education and efforts to reduce them. Throughout her career, each endeavor has been driven by the hope that trustworthy evidence can inform and compel more equitable policy and practice. She turned to the idea of *public scholarship* as it became increasingly clear that knowledge production alone is insufficient to ameliorate deeply entrenched social inequalities. Anthony is freshly embarking on his career as an education researcher, bringing years of experience as a teacher in a system that daily exhibited the human costs of unequal education and philosophical training that enabled him to co-construct the emancipatory possibilities of a humanities-based curriculum with his students.

Our partnership began in the context of planning for the American Educational Research Association's (AERA) annual meeting in 2016—the association's centennial year. As president, Jeannie was charged with developing a theme that would allow us to celebrate, reflect, and anticipate our second century of education research. Anthony served as a key member of the AERA annual meeting planning team. With an outstanding group of colleagues, we sought ways for the annual meeting to recall the social, democratic and academic aspirations that gave rise to our research community 100 years ago.[1]

We gained inspiration from those earliest scholars who envisioned the role of social science in helping to strengthen society's most democratic institution—public education—to ensure the continued vitality of a democratic society. Throughout our planning, we were humbled by how far our profession and society have fallen short of those hopes.

Over the past century, scholars have sought scientific knowledge to improve large, increasingly diverse education systems. Nonetheless, an array of current sociopolitical inequalities bears uncanny resemblances to those of 1916. Now, as then, education provides the terrain through which our nation's deepest anxieties and fears are manifested, and social research has had seemingly little impact on the intertwined ills that lie at the root of these conditions. Throughout this history, much research that may have empowered our diverse democracy by informing educational practice has remained unexplored, superficially understood, or unheeded.[2] From this history, one conclusion stands out: striving for equitable, inclusive education requires as much attention to public perceptions and multileveled politics as to professional science. No matter how praised research may be in professional ranks, it is often overpowered in national discourse by dominant cultural norms and politics.

Drawing from the history of education research, our planning team sought insights for ways to improve our profession for the greater vitality and equality of our democracy. John Dewey's precept for researchers to act as *public scholars* shaped our thinking, and by celebrating scholars who've "gone public," we hoped to spark a critical imagining of ways to create and support educational equity in the century to come.

Tradition and Current Opportunities

We advanced a view of public scholars as those who engage multiple publics through reflexive means and at different levels. We highlighted those who partner with non-academics to explore the complex linkages among science, technology, history, and the cultural norms and everyday politics that shape our educational landscape. We sought to highlight how public scholars achieve this by working with *dominant publics* (in policymaking arenas and elsewhere), as well as with *counterpublics*—groups with subordinate status whose interests and experiences are frequently excluded from everyday discourse (Dawson 2006; Fraser 1990; Warner 2002). By helping to identify and frame urgent educational problems as collective matters rather than individual concerns, public scholars strive to engender democratic participation through collaborative research. Drawing from a century of successes and failures, we called for researchers to learn from the ways that research has helped transform discriminatory and exclusionary ideas about education into equitable, meaningful changes.

Our own preparations routinely drew from Jane Addams (2002), W. E. B. Du Bois (1996, 1999), and John Dewey (1980, 1984), who envisioned a thoroughly *social* science that, above all else, should function as a public good. This academic legacy continues to cast new light on old lessons about the relationships among research, publics, and social change. It is a reminder that understanding educational problems and devising solutions requires local knowledge and inclusive participation that transcends the limits of researchers' expertise. We recognize that Dewey, Addams, and Du Bois ultimately fell short of elevating the public weal, and although the contemporary public sphere is rife with social and political tumult, we believe there is reason for much greater optimism today. Unlike then, our field is not under the near-exclusive guidance of White men, and our diverse array of scholars and epistemologies more closely reflects the technical, cultural, and political struggles of educating our diverse democracy. We are frequently reminded of Dewey's insistence that democracy is always a task *before* us; successes and failures are always provisional, and researchers must be capable of adapting to changing social, political, and economic conditions that shape education and society.

The opaque and highly contentious political conditions of the present provide ideal opportunities for public scholarship. As Biesta (2007) points out, periods of sociopolitical consensus regarding the purposes of education relegate the role of research to technical ends alone. During such times, public demands for research mostly reflect desires for better ways of counting and measuring—areas we have proudly made great advances in. However, a lack of consensus creates opportunities for research to play a role that exceeds technical expertise. Public scholarship can play a cultural role in shaping dominant beliefs and attitudes about education, thereby providing the catalyst for alleviating educational inequality in the next century of research.

Engagement and Translation: Key Dimensions of Public Scholarship

In our view, the twin elements of *engagement* and *translation* lie at the heart of public scholarship. As educators know well, building relationships through active engagement is a key modality of knowledge construction for both novices and experts. Likewise, communicating research findings and implications to multiple publics in accessible, useful forms inevitably tests and clarifies the knowledge itself. What follows are further explorations—ideas in progress—for engagement and translation in public scholarship to add value to the quality and impact of education research in the twenty-first century. We hope that researchers take up these suggestions, while readily admitting our own lack of knowledge about the ways that engagement, translation, and the production and uses of research can bring multiple publics together, linked by the belief in education as a public good.

Engagement

Public scholarship is underscored by the belief that our most profound educational problems are not amenable to "engineering" solutions and technical approaches alone cannot counter the broad structures that are themselves shaped by dominant values and beliefs. From Dewey, Addams, and Du Bois, we inherit a legacy of what Michael Burawoy (2005) calls *organic* public scholars—those who work directly and collaboratively with non-academics to solve immediate, concrete problems related to education. In operational terms, engagement means working within an ecosystem that produces, uses, and disseminates knowledge in concert with broader struggles for cultural change and political shifts (Oakes forthcoming). Researchers can help non-academics normalize the methods of social inquiry by working within what Dewey called the "hurly burly" of everyday life to understand and collectively confront the unequal conditions our publics face (Dewey 1985; Oakes and Rogers 2006). By empowering our publics' capacities for social inquiry, engagement is a powerful means of transforming commonsense approaches to educational inequality, reframing matters as *collective* rather than *individual* problems (Dewey 1984; Oakes forthcoming; Stikkers 2010).

While engagement can be conceived as a set of relational strategies for communicating and collaborating with those outside the academy, it suggests a new set of relationships within institutions of higher education as well. In the face of an unprecedented and unknowable future for American education, researchers must do everything we can to assure our publics of our commitment to accessible, high-quality education as a public good, and to do so in explicitly political and value-laden terms. We can do this by helping our publics publicly reject policies and practices of exclusion, segregation, and deprivation that leave so many students and communities with a deep distrust of educational institutions. We can do this by employing value-laden language that offers not merely a normative vision but a practical pathway to realize equitable and exemplary education for all students. Though inward-facing debates about epistemological orientations and methods strengthen our field in vital ways, they are far from our most urgent problems as researchers. And while the norms of scientific objectivity are helpful in maintaining rigorous standards, they provide no justification for remaining apolitical given our current state.

Engagement can also provide a lens for rethinking how we collaborate with colleagues inside research communities. Engagement is not the province of any single type of research alone, and researchers who do not come into direct contact with non-academics can substantially contribute to public scholarship in important ways. As increasing racial and ethnic diversity brings about new ways of knowing, hybrid methodologies can help academic discourse adapt and can strengthen our societal relevance. We are thinking here of Shepard's (2016) call for future experts in counting and measuring to develop not only quantitative skills, but also deep understandings of the constructs and contexts of schooling that reflect evolving conceptions of knowledge and practice. Similarly, Lee (2016) argues that the challenges of bridging theory and practice require widespread institutionalization of interdisciplinary collaborations that are capable of responding to changing conditions and diminishing educational opportunities. By strengthening our methodological base, such partnerships can buffer critics who fear that extra-academic partnerships threaten our professional standards. Interdisciplinary and public partnerships of this sort promise to enrich research knowledge by expanding its locus of production and vetting *without* compromising the scholarly rigor and symbolic capital necessary to gain traction in public domains.

Decades ago, Charles Payne warned of the deleterious effects of devaluing direct engagement with non-academics for the sake of professional reward. Considering how the current risks and rewards of public scholarship defy professional convention, his words are prescient so long as peer-reviewed journal publications are disproportionately valued over the lives affected by scholarly public engagement. Failure to engage our publics would result, he wrote, in "[the] inability to consider things from a variety of perspectives, the refusal to consider them holistically, [which] is partly a function of professional vanity, vanity that limits us to doing research *on* people rather than *with* them or *for* them" (Payne 1984, 183). While working democratically and publicly to produce knowledge that furthers the aims of educational justice, we must make every effort to ensure the soundness, clarity, and trustworthiness of our research. In this light, engaging with publics *raises* the expectation for high-quality research rather than diminishing it. The stakes are too high for anything less.

Translation

If the success of public scholarship depends on the degree to which researchers are able to work in concert with broader equity-focused struggles, equally determinative is the ability to translate research expertise in ways that are both useful and understandable for our publics by employing organic and relational strategies. This translation occurs when the hurly burly of everyday life facilitates unmediated dialogue between researchers and education professionals, students, community actors, and others as they collaboratively investigate their immediate problems and develop useful solutions. In many cases, efforts to translate research findings are aimed primarily at policymakers—an important task, to be sure, but one that will not transform commonsense societal beliefs about education. History shows that the energies propelling justice-oriented social change will come neither from the academy nor from policymakers alone, but rather from those in the midst of enduring existing inequalities.

Employing lexicons and communication strategies that are commonly understood remains a primary challenge of public scholarship. Consider how, from the start, researchers are guided toward peer-reviewed journals and academic conferences, and lauded for mastery of arcane language that signifies specialization. Training in professional standards is certainly essential for the vitality of our field, though in many cases it further isolates us from the publics we wish to engage. If "the fruit of communication should be participation" (Dewey 1958, 166), the fruit we bear exists almost entirely within the rarefied air of elite, exclusive spaces. Scholars are rewarded for conducting research "about" problems related to education, whereby groups in question frequently become objects of scientific study rather than equal partners capable of expressing their democratic subjectivity. Still, scholars are commonly frustrated as their work continues to be inaccessible or undesirable for the publics they want to reach. Graduate training and professional reward structures remain monumental obstacles to this model of public scholarship, and though we lack space here for a more thorough analysis of this issue, it remains an area in need of further research.

Until these professional aspects of public scholarship are addressed, we can only urge future scholarship to heed the social fact that research is not self-enacting. Diverse actors must feel a sense of ownership in the knowledge produced and contextualize it in a way that fosters dispositions to credibly inform others and collectively press for changes in policy or practice. Researchers should locate and operate within widely used public venues, and future research can examine the co-evolution of successful communication strategies and changing relationships between people and information. Many scholars are already adept at writing for broad audiences through op-eds, blogs, and other emerging media, future and junior scholars should be encouraged to learn from those already engaged in these activities. Such encouragement must be matched, however, with recognition and professional reward for these aspects of researchers' work.

When scholars are able to use their expertise in this way, the translation function of public scholarship can *create* publics. By attending to and learning from the ways that cultural norms and political power shift over time, scholars can better understand how research is framed in ways that resonate with mainstream audiences, which in turn can shape educational policy and practice in equitable directions. As Welner (2012) argues, judicial rulings and litigation outcomes are significantly affected by prevailing sentiments in the public sphere. In this light, researchers should attend to the politicization of public beliefs about science overall and education in particular. Gauchat (2012) has shown that in recent decades, identification with conservative ideologies has been the strongest determinant of opposition to any interdependence of organized science and government policy. As a starting point to examine how equity-focused research can negotiate with social ontologies that refute established knowledge brokers (such as academics), the translation function of public scholarship can seek new avenues to communicate the normative and collective goals of equitable education alongside, not in lieu of, empirical findings.

To bridge ideological divides, public scholars can foster evidence-based narratives whose meanings are broadly understood and shared (Oakes forthcoming). Public scholars must work continuously to help our publics communicate their stories in a way that demands attention in the dominant public sphere. These narratives—driven by the lived experiences of affected publics and informed by rigorous research—are capable of attaining special claims on policymakers' attention precisely because they are grounded in empirical evidence (Marris 1997). Drawing these together, public scholars can help these narratives find new audiences in policy, professional, and public spheres, while appealing to activists and advocates who share equity-focused aims. Evidence-based narratives differ from evidence-based policies, as the latter may take questions of educational ends to be given, focusing solely on questions of which means are most "effective" in a given setting. Without interrogating educational ends or encouraging deliberations about the purpose of a given practice, such policies may ultimately do little to change societal values or beliefs. By facilitating critical inquiry of this kind, evidence-based narratives are the primary mechanism for public scholarship to transcend the *technical* uses of education research by enacting a *cultural* role. In this sense, translation may utilize communication strategies of popular narratives as a vital counterpart to strategies known to be effective with policy audiences. Most publics are not conversant in the language of policy, educational or otherwise, and yet nearly all members participate in the social and cultural (re)production of narratives that inform policy and shape societal values and beliefs about *who* can learn and *what* they can learn. The actual *meaning* of any evidence-based narrative is determined not by researchers, but by the publics who co-construct them. As Payne might suggest, we succumb to professional vanity if we insist otherwise.

Public Scholarship: A Common Cause for Education Researchers

As researchers, we *all* have the choice to engage in or support public scholarship. This isn't to say that all graduate students and established scholars ought to throw themselves headfirst into public engagement. Many scholars have skills, preferences, and substantive work that don't bring them into direct contact with non-academic publics. However, researchers working in policy, professional, or critical realms *can* support colleagues who want to engage non-academic publics. More broadly, all members of the academic community can recognize and help to mitigate institutional barriers for scholars who want to act publicly but are constrained by limited training opportunities, promotion and reward systems, and (academic) cultural biases that discourage public engagement.

Toward this end, it is helpful to return to the central questions of social research that Michael Burawoy illuminated in his 2005 presidential address to the American Sociological Association: *for whom* and *for what* do we pursue academic knowledge? These questions remind us that education has always been a public good in the United States, and it is our duty to ensure that education research, through public scholarship, recommits itself as a powerful agent for that public good. To provisionally answer Burawoy's questions: We pursue education research for those youth and communities who are most affected by large-scale, unjust arrangements. Far from being a panacea, public scholarship is a flexible and adaptive framework for education researchers to pursue solutions to these unjust arrangements.

NOTES

1. The team also included Kevin Welner, Michelle Renee Valladares, Michael Harris, and Katherine Wiley, all from the University of Colorado Boulder.

2. Certainly, not *all* education-related social science fits into this category; some has been wrong and dangerous, and we are glad to see its demise.

REFERENCES

Addams, Jane. 2002. *The long road of woman's memory.* Champaign: University of Illinois Press.

Biesta, Gert. 2007. "Why 'what works' won't work: evidence-based practice and the democratic deficit in education research." *Educational Theory* 57: 1–22.

Burawoy, Michael. 2005. "For public sociology." *American Sociological Review* 70: 4–28.

Dawson, Michael C. 2006. "After the deluge: Publics and publicity in Katrina's wake." *Du Bois Review* 3: 239–49.

Dewey, John. 1958. *Experience and nature.* New York: Dover Publications.

Dewey, John. 1980. "Democracy and education." In *The middle works, 1899–1924,* vol. 9, edited by J. A. Boydston, 1–370. Carbondale: Southern Illinois University Press.

Dewey, John. 1984. "The public and its problems." In *The later works, 1925–1953,* vol. 2, edited by J. A. Boydston, 235–372. Carbondale: Southern Illinois University Press.

Dewey, John. 1985. "Is there hope for politics?" In *The later works, 1925–1952,* vol. 6, edited by J. A. Boydston, 182–89. Carbondale: Southern Illinois University Press.

Du Bois, W. E. B. 1996. *The Philadelphia Negro: A social study.* Philadelphia: University of Pennsylvania Press.

Du Bois, W. E. B. 1999. *Darkwater: Voices from within the veil.* Mineola, NY: Dover Publications.

Fraser, Nancy. 1990. "Rethinking the public sphere: A contribution to the critique of actually existing democracy." *Social Text* 25/26: 56–80.

Gauchat, Gordon. 2012. "Politicization of science in the public sphere: A study of public trust in the United States, 1974 to 2010." *American Sociological Review* 77: 167–87.

Lee, Carol D. 2016. "Examining conceptions of how people learn over the decades through AERA presidential addresses: Diversity and equity as persistent conundrums." *Educational Researcher* 45: 73–82.

Marris, Peter. 1997. *Witnesses, engineers, or storytellers: Using research for social policy and community action.* College Park: University of Maryland, Urban Studies and Planning Program.

Oakes, Jeannie. Forthcoming. "Public scholarship: Education research for diverse democracies." *Educational Researcher.*

Oakes, Jeannie, and John Rogers. 2006. *Learning power: Organizing for education and justice.* New York: Teachers College Press.

Payne, Charles. 1984. *Getting what we ask for: The ambiguity of success and failure in urban education.* Westport, CT: Greenwood Press.

Shepard, Lorrie A. 2016. "Testing and assessment for the good of education: Contributions of AERA presidents, 1915–2015." *Educational Researcher* 45: 112–21.

Stikkers, Kenneth W. 2010. "John Dewey on the public responsibility of intellectuals." *Ethics and Politics* 12: 195–206.

Warner, Michael. 2002. "Publics and counterpublics," *Public Culture* 14: 49–90.

Welner, Kevin G. 2012. "Scholars as policy actors: Research, public discourse, and the zone of judicial constraints." *American Educational Research Journal* 49: 7–29.

Editor

LAURA W. PERNA is the James S. Riepe Professor and executive director of the Alliance for Higher Education and Democracy at the University of Pennsylvania (Penn), as well as past president of the Association for the Study of Higher Education and chair of Penn's faculty senate. She is also a fellow of the American Educational Research Association. Her research focuses on identifying how social structures, educational practices, and public policies can promote college access and success, particularly for groups that continue to be underrepresented in higher education. Her recent books include *The Attainment Agenda: State Policy Leadership for Higher Education* (with Joni Finney, 2014) and *The State of College Access and Completion: Improving College Success for Students from Underrepresented Groups* (with Anthony Jones, 2013).

Contributors

ANN E. AUSTIN is a professor of higher, adult, and lifelong education and associate dean for research in the College of Education, and assistant provost for faculty development—academic career paths at Michigan State University. Austin's research concerns faculty careers and professional development, teaching and learning in higher education, the academic workplace, organizational change, doctoral education, and reform in STEM (science, technology, engineering, and mathematics) education. Her books include *Faculty Development in the Age of Evidence: Current Practices, Future Imperatives* (with A. Beach, M. D. Sorcinelli, and J. Rivard, 2016), and *Rethinking Faculty Work: Higher Education's Strategic Imperative* (with J. Gappa and A. Trice, 2007).

ESTELA MARA BENSIMON is founding director of the Center for Urban Education (CUE) and a professor at the University of Southern California. Her current research is on racial equity in higher education from the perspective of organizational learning and sociocultural practice theories. Recent publications include *Engaging the Race Question: Accountability and Equity in US Higher Education* (with Alicia C. Dowd) and *Critical Approaches to the Study of Higher Education* (with Ana Martínez-Alemán and Brian Pusser). Her opinion pieces have been published in *Inside Higher Ed, Denver Post, Sacramento Bee*, and *Zocalo.*

ANTHONY A. BERRYMAN is a PhD student at the University of California at Los Angeles's Graduate School of Education and Information Studies. A former English and philosophy teacher at Compton High School, Berryman's interests include the relationships among equity-focused policy reforms, democratic education, and strategies aimed at engaging and empowering urban youth, teachers, and community members. A high school dropout, Berryman was an integral part of the all-ages music scene in Los Angeles for several years before returning to education. His forthcoming dissertation examines strategies of public scholars from varying ideological orientations and sociopolitical contexts, and the impact of their strategies in policy arenas.

MITCHELL J. CHANG is a professor of higher education and organizational change and Asian American Studies (by courtesy) at the University of California, Los Angeles (UCLA). Chang's research focuses on diversity-related issues and initiatives on college campuses. He has written over ninety publications, some of which have been cited in US Supreme Court rulings concerning the use of race-conscious admissions practices.

CHERYL CRAZY BULL, a citizen of the Sicangu Lakota Nation, focuses her scholarship on advocacy for the indigenous voice in academia, in research, and in telling the story of Native people in the United States. As president of the American Indian College Fund, she strives to increase access to and success in postsecondary education, including research and scholarship opportunities for all Native students. Her recent publications focus on the identity of tribal colleges, presidential leadership at tribal colleges, and tribal self-determination strategies, such as tribal college governance and the development of indigenous studies. She promotes the development of data, technology, and research capacity among tribal nations and organizations to increase the ability of tribal people to tell their own story, in their own words, and with their own evaluation of their success.

ADAM GAMORAN is president of the William T. Grant Foundation, a charitable organization celebrating its eightieth year of supporting research to improve the lives of young people. Previously he was a professor of sociology and educational policy studies at the University of Wisconsin–Madison, where he chaired the sociology department and directed the Wisconsin Center for Education Research. He co-edited *Stratification in Higher Education: A Comparative Study* (2007) and has published widely on educational inequality and school reform.

SARA GOLDRICK-RAB is a professor of higher education policy and sociology at Temple University. As a scholar-activist she examines ways to integrate higher education and social policies to increase college attainment. In 2013, she founded the Wisconsin HOPE Lab, the nation's only translational research laboratory aimed at making college affordable. *Politico* magazine named her one of the top fifty people shaping American politics, and she worked with both the Obama Administration and state legislatures on approaches to making college free. Her most recent book is *Paying the Price: College Costs, Financial Aid, and the Betrayal of the American Dream* (2016).

SHAUN R. HARPER is a provost professor in the Rossier School of Education and the Marshall School of Business at the University of Southern California. He also is the Clifford and Betty Allen Chair in Urban Leadership, executive director of the USC Race and Equity Center, and former president of the Association for the Study of Higher Education. His research focuses on equity, racial climates, and racialized experiences in educational and organizational contexts. Harper spent a decade on the faculty at the University of Pennsylvania, where he founded the Center for the Study of Race and Equity in Education.

DONALD E. HELLER is provost and vice president of academic affairs and a professor of education at the University of San Francisco. He is responsible for the university's five schools, libraries, academic affairs, student life, enrollment management, online programs, and international relations, and diversity and community outreach for the university's 11,000 students and 2,200 faculty and staff. His teaching and research are in the areas of educational economics, public policy, and finance, with a primary focus on issues of college access, choice, and success for low-income and minority students. He is the editor of five books, including most recently *Student Financing of Higher Education: A Comparative Perspective* (with C. Callender, 2013).

ADRIANNA KEZAR is a professor at the University of Southern California and co-director of the Pullias Center for Higher Education. Her research focuses on change, governance, and leadership in higher education and the changing faculty, including how to better support adjunct faculty. Recent publications include *How Colleges Change* (2013), *Enhancing Campus Capacity for Leadership* (2011), and *Embracing Non-Tenure Track Faculty* (2012).

SIMON MARGINSON is a professor of international higher education at the Institute of Education, University College London, and director of the ESRC/HEFCE Centre for Global Higher Education. He is also joint editor-in-chief of the journal *Higher Education*. His work is primarily focused on global and international aspects of higher education, and problems of higher education and social inequality. His books include *The Dream Is Over: The Crisis of Clark Kerr's California Idea of Higher Education* (2016) and *Higher Education and the Common Good* (2016).

JAMES T. MINOR is senior strategist for academic success at the California State University (CSU) Chancellor's Office. CSU is the largest and most diverse four-year system of higher education in the nation, enrolling more than 475,000 students. Prior to joining CSU, James served as deputy assistant secretary at the US Department of Education, overseeing $7.8 billion dollars of federal programming intended to advance college access, degree completion, and innovation. In his former position as associate professor of higher education at Michigan State University, his scholarship focused higher education policy, academic governance, and institutional performance.

JEANNIE OAKES is Presidential Professor in Education Equity, Emeritus, at UCLA's Graduate School of Education and Information Studies, and senior fellow in residence at the Learning Policy Institute. In 2014, she completed a six-year term at the Ford Foundation as director of educational opportunity and scholarship programs. Oakes's research examines inequalities in US schools and follows the progress of equity reform. This work is the subject of *Keeping Track: How Schools Structure Inequality* (2005), *Becoming Good American Schools: The Struggle for Civic Virtue in Education Reform* (2002), *Learning Power: Organizing for Education and Justice* (2006), and *Teaching to Change the World* (2015).

GARY RHOADES is a professor and director of the University of Arizona's Center for the Study of Higher Education. Rhoades's work concentrates on the restructuring of academic institutions and professions, as in *Managed Professionals: Unionized Faculty and the Restructuring of Academic Labor* (1998), and *Academic Capitalism and the New Economy: Markets, State, and Higher Education* (with Sheila Slaughter, 2004).

DANIEL G. SOLORZANO is a professor of social science and comparative education in the Graduate School of Education and Information Studies at the University of California, Los Angeles. His teaching and research interests include critical race theory in education, racial microaggressions and other forms of everyday racism, critical race spatial analysis, and critical race pedagogy. Solorzano has authored over 100 research articles and book chapters. His recent publications include "Racial Microaggressions as a Tool for Critical Race Research," in *Race, Ethnicity, and Education*; "Using Critical Race Spatial Analysis to Examine the Du Boisian Color-Line Along the Alameda Corridor in Southern California," in the *Whittier Law Review*; and "Teaching Racial Microaggressions: Implications of Critical Race Hypos for Social Work," in the *Journal of Ethnic & Cultural Diversity in Social Work*.

CHRISTINE A. STANLEY is professor of higher education and vice president and associate provost for diversity at Texas A&M University. She previously served as acting vice provost for academic affairs, executive associate dean for faculty affairs in the College of Education and Human Development, and associate dean of faculties. Her research interests are faculty professional development and diversity and social justice in higher education. She co-authored the Standards of Professional Practice for Chief Diversity Officers, and she is a recipient of the Mildred Garcia Award for Exemplary Scholarship for a Senior-Practitioner Scholar from ASHE and the named Christine A. Stanley Award for Diversity and Inclusion Research in Educational Development from the Professional and Organizational Development Network in Higher Education.

WILLIAM G. TIERNEY is a university professor, the Wilbur-Kieffer Professor of Higher Education, and co-director of the Pullias Center for Higher Education at the University of Southern California, as well as past president of the American Educational Research Association (AERA). His research focuses on increasing access to higher education, improving the performance of post-secondary institutions, and analyzing the impact of privatization on post-secondary education. He is a fellow of AERA and a member of the National Academy of Education. His most recent book is *Rethinking Education and Poverty* (2015). He has had Fulbright fellowships to Central America, Australia, and most recently, India. He is looking at issues of privatization, academic freedom, access to higher education for low-income students, institutional quality, and academic corruption.